AF539830

LEADERSHIP STYLES AND SHURA SYSTEM

An Islamic Perspective

LEADERSHIP STYLES AND SHURA SYSTEM

An Islamic Perspective

DR. MOHAMMED GALIB HUSSAIN
Associate Professor and Head, Department of Corporate Secretaryship
Islamiah College, Vaniyambadi (T.N.)

and

DR. M. AKBAR MOHIDEEN
Associate Professor, Department of Corporate Secretaryship
C. Abdul Hakeem College, Melvisharam (T.N.)

DEEP & DEEP PUBLICATIONS PVT. LTD.
F-159, Rajouri Garden, New Delhi - 110 027

LEADERSHIP STYLES AND SHURA SYSTEM
An Islamic Perspective

ISBN 978-81-8450-299-2

Printed in India at MAYUR ENTERPRISES
WZ Plot No. 3, Gujjar Market, Tihar Village, New Delhi - 110 018

Published by DEEP & DEEP PUBLICATIONS PVT. LTD.,
F-159, Rajouri Garden, New Delhi - 110 027 • Phone : 25435369, 25440916
E-mail : ddpubs@gmail.com • ddpbooks@yahoo.co.in
Showroom :
2/13, Ansari Road, Daryaganj, New Delhi - 110 002 • Telefax : 23245122

DEDICATION

Perpetual merit (Sawab-e-Jaria) for the deceased

Dad :
Shaik Jamal

Mom :
Hamidunnisa

Wife :
Mumtaj Begum

By
Mohammed Galib Hussain

Dad :
M. Mohammed Meeran

By
M. Akbar Mohideen

Contents

Preface

Leadership is the decisive factor in human affairs. Hence the leader is a basic necessity of a society. Leadership is both a role and a process of influencing others. The true spirit of leadership is to give and not to take. It is about caring and supporting without expecting to be cared and supported. It is about being just with even those who are not fair. It is about spreading order out of chaos, creating confidence out of despair, trust out of suspicion and courage out of fear.

There is a copious literature developed by western authors on the subject. The output of research in this area is quite phenomenal. Psychologists, organizational behaviour theorists and business management thinkers have expanded horizons of knowledge by articulating theories which are logically sound and intuitively appealing. Needless to say these are the products of human mind. Islam is a revealed religion for the entire mankind preserved in pristine form of revealed book of Allah the Quran and Divine Inspired sayings and doings of Prophet Muhammad. Rightly guided companions of Prophet Muhammad and noble souls have left precepts and practices which constitute a rich material of Islam. There is a need to understand the phenomenon of leadership in the light of Divine Guidance.

An attempt has been made in this work to cull out all those leadership traits prescribed by the divinity. The Divine Guidance has elaborated a detailed mechanism of mutual consultation system *(Shura)* for decision-making. The authors have described the nuts and bolts of this process; differences between western leadership styles and *Shura* system have been brought out in this research work. The unique features of Islamic theory of leadership are articulated.

An interesting and an inspiring insight about ethical behaviour and moral bases of leadership form an Islamic perspective. Leadership in Islam is a trust. It represents a psychological agreement between a leader and his followers that he will try his level best to guide them, protect them and treat them fairly with justice. Islamic Leadership style is a unique style which includes consensus building traits such as *Shura* (mutual consultation).

The study offers a solution to the leadership problems faced by Muslims and non-Muslims in an organizational framework. Verses from the Holy Book; words and deeds of the Prophet; life history and practical incidents are illustrated.

We wish to express our heartfelt thanks to all those writers whose works we have consulted. Their contributions to the development of thought in this book have been acknowledged by way of citations where ever needed. It is quite possible that some of the ideas, views and conclusions of some authorities on Islam might have influenced, albeit sub-consciously, our thinking. To all of them, we shall ever remain indebted.

The managements, the former as well as the present Secretaries, the Principals—current and the past—of Islamiah College, Vaniyambadi and C. Abdul Hakeem College, Melvisharam have shown keen interest in the project. Janab S. Ziauddin Saheb, Chairman, Melvisharam Muslim Educational Society, Melvisharam and Janab C. Khaiser Ahmed Saheb, Secretary and Correspondent, Islamiah College, Vaniyambadi have taken personal interest in the study. We express our sincere gratitude to all of them.

We would like place on record our deep appreciation of excellent work of Mr. G.S. Bhatia and his team at Deep and Deep Publications Pvt. Ltd. in bringing out this book in such a beautiful getup.

DR. MOHAMMED GALIB HUSSAIN
DR. M. AKBAR MOHIDEEN

1

Introduction

In the name of Allah, Most Gracious, Most Merciful.

"And We made them leaders guiding (men) by Our command and We sent them inspiration to do good deeds, to establish regular prayers and to practice regular charity; and they constantly served Us (and Us only)".

—(Quran 21: 73)

"It is part of the Mercy of Allah that thou dost deal gently with them. Wert thou severe or harsh-hearted, they would have broken away from about thee: so pass over (their faults), and ask for (Allah's) forgiveness for them; and consult them in affairs (of moment) then, when thou hast taken a decision, put thy trust in Allah for Allah loves those who put their trust (in Him)".

—(Quran 3: 159)

MORAL DIMENSIONS

Leadership is the decisive factor in human affairs. Hence, we may say that the leader is a basic necessity of a society. In these days of modernity, the society cannot much depend on the imbibed leadership qualities. The society is bound to evolve and develop into a model system, mechanism and culture through which capable and meritorious persons may emerge as able leaders. Leadership is both a role and a process of influencing others.

The true spirit of leadership is to give, and not to take. It is about caring without expecting to be cared about. It is about supporting without expecting to be supported. It is about being just with even those who are not fair. Leadership is about giving followers the missing dimensions. It is about spreading order out of chaos; creating confidence out of despair, trust out of suspicion and courage out of fear. Leadership is about making changes. Leaders do not necessarily hold positions of authority. They neither drive their influence from wealth nor from power. The most successful leader is one who leads, without the followers even knowing that they are being led. Ultimately, when the leader's values are transferred, the follower must say they are his own values. Eventually, when he develops total confidence in the leader, he must feel he has developed confidence in himself. When he finally begins to live under the guidance of the leader, he must feel he is living under his own guidance. This is the final victory of a leader.

Of late, there had been a growing concern that Western theories of leadership styles have not been effective. These styles, which have been given very long trial in many organizations, have proved to be ineffective. From this point of view, we do not find such systems or mechanisms existing in other "isms". When we study Islam we find that a true follower of Islam will have the quality to emerge as a leader in every situation. Islam is a complete way of life, in which every aspect of human behaviour has been explained in the light of Quran and Sunnah.

Leadership in Islam is a trust. Often it takes the form of an explicit contract or pledge between a leader and his followers that he will try his best to guide them, to protect them and treat them fairly with justice. Hence, the focus of leadership in Islam is on integrity and justice. Given the recent emphasis on ethical behaviour in the leadership literature, an examination of the moral bases of leadership from an Islamic perspective may flash some interesting insights in the field of leadership.

In Islam, teachings and practices are so excellently designed that a true follower of Islam is capable of becoming a leader. Islam says that man is superior to all creatures and he is born to rule this material world. This very concept guides a Muslim to obtain the status of a leader in the group (Maududi, 1991). One who follows the Islamic principles is bestowed with leadership qualities. One of many such examples in Islamic history; a simple conqueror like Mohamed Bin Quasim was rated high even by his enemies in Sindh due to his benevolent behaviour. We also find in history that all great men were impressed or inspired by some other great men of their time. It is but a natural phenomenon. In Islam it is essential to believe Prophet Mohamed (Sal) as a guide, leader and Spiritual head. He is an ideal model not only for the Muslims but also the richest blessing to the entire humanity. *"O, Mohamed, we have not sent you but as a blessing for all the worlds"*. (Quran 21: 107)

It is very interesting to see that Michael H. Hart in his famous book, "The 100: A ranking of the Most Influential Persons in History", chooses Prophet Mohamed (Sal) as "number one". Dr. Hart says, "My choice of Mohamed to lead the list of the world's most influential persons may surprise some readers and may be questioned by others, but he was the only man in history who was supremely successful on both religious and secular levels".

Islamic principles of management emphasize a higher system of morality by virtue of which people can realize their potentiality. It purifies the soul from self-seeking egoism, tyranny, wantonness and indiscipline. It creates God-fearing men, devoted to their ideal, possessed with piety, abstinence, and discipline and uncompromising in the face of truth. It induces feeling of moral responsibility and boosts the capacity of self-control. It generates kindness, generosity, mercy, sympathy, peace, disinterested good will, scrupulous fairness and truthfulness towards everybody in all situations. It nourishes noble qualities from which only good may be expected.

Allah, the Almighty, created human beings, equiped them with the faculty of intellect, and made this whole universe subservient to them. This means that Allah provided mankind with both skills and resources. Some people and nations obtained more success than others did in using what Allah has given them. The degree of success of nations depends largely on their leadership and their motivation. Muslims have achieved a historically unique success. Currently, the countries and the organisations that are showing rapid growth are the ones that are privileged with better leadership.

The performance of an organization is very much influenced by the quality of its leadership. The leader should assume the overall responsibility of the organization. Further, leadership should be understood more as a service to the organization and its members. The saying of Prophet Mohamed (Sal) supports this understanding, which is compatible with TQM concepts. The Prophet (Sal) said, *"The leader of people is their servant"* (Tabrani). Leadership is necessary for the success of any collective work as evident in the saying of the Prophet (Sal), *"If there were three in a trip, they shall appoint a leader from among them"* (Abu Dawood). Islam thus approves the utility of leadership.

Thus the religious philosophy behind Islam has a universal application and has no rituals attached and can be adopted by anyone who seeks perfection in a certain way prescribed in the source book [*Quran*] and the practices of Prophet Mohamed (Sal) [*Sunnah*]. Based on the above facts and moral dimensions of true leadership, this study focuses on what leadership is from an Islamic point of view, and discusses the characteristics of leaders and followers, as suggested by Islam and analyses the *Shura* (mutual consultation) system in Islamic culture.

The pronoun "he" has been used throughout this study in a generic sense, so as the word "Muslim" to include both male and female. Likewise, the words "subordinates" and "followers" have been used synonymously. The names of the authors whose writings have been referred are presented at the end of the chapters to facilitate readability. All Islamic and/or Arabic terms are explained in the glossary.

STATEMENT OF THE PROBLEM

The Western theories of leadership followed not only by the Muslim leaders but also by many others have proved to be ineffective, which necessitate the search for a universally applicable theory. This has been further emphasised by the current reemergence of the universal Islamic identity. This search for roots inevitably leads to a revisit of Islamic theory of leadership.

This study tries to show that Islam, as a way of life, is compatible as well as an effective force in the process of management. More specifically, the need for this study stems from the following facts:

- that Western models of leadership do not prove helpful when transplanted to other socio-cultural environments;
- that the Islamic literature pertaining to the topic under study needs to be articulated;
- that the Autocratic style of leadership, which is followed in many organizations, has proved to be ineffective, and Islamic theory of leadership can rectify the same;
- that the Democratic as well as Bureaucratic style of leadership seems to be more suitable in theory, but take the role of autocracy in practice;
- that an Islamic system of leadership (based on *Shura*) offers a viable alternative to Western model;
- that the Shura system, though it resembles Democratic style of leadership, is different from the latter in practice; and
- that the characteristics of a leader as propounded by the Creator (the God) in the Quran and practiced by His messenger, Prophet Mohamed (Sal), have universal applicability:

OBJECTIVES OF THE STUDY

In the light of the above facts, this study has the following objectives:

- to identify the pattern of management style in Islamic culture;
- to explain the characteristics of effective leaders in general, and of Islamic leaders in particular;

- to describe Shura system and explain its applicability in the business organisational context;
- to formulate Islamic theory of leadership and to explain its unique features; and
- to bring out the differences between Western conceptualization of leadership styles and Islamic conceptualization of leadership styles.

MEANING AND DEFINITION OF THE TERMS

The terms, which constitute the title of the thesis "Leadership Style and Shura System in Islamic Culture", are defined and elucidated here for the purpose of understanding.

Leader : A leader is a member of a group who is given a certain rank and is expected to perform in a manner consistent with that rank. Also, a leader is the person who is expected to exercise influence in forming and accomplishing the group's goals. An honest leader is the one who leads and not the one who manipulates to lead.

Leadership : Leadership can be defined as the capacity to mobilise a group of people towards a set of articulated goals and ensure their continuous co-operation for realisation of these goals. Leadership refers to the process of moving people in a planned direction by motivating them to action through non-compulsive means. Good leadership moves people in a direction that the means and ends should serve the best interests of the people involved in a real and long-term sense. Some more definitions of leadership given by prominent authorities are stated below:

- "Leadership is the relationship in which one person, the leader, influences others to work together willingly on related tasks to attain that which the leader desires".

  —*George O. Terry*
- "Leadership is the interpersonal influence, exercised in situations and directed, through the communication process, towards the attainment of goals".

  —*Tannenbaum*
- "Leadership is the process by which the leader seeks

the voluntary participation of followers in an effort to reach organisational objectives". —*Schriescheim*

- "Leadership is the ability to persuade others to seek defined objectives enthusiastically. It is the human factor which binds a group together and motivates it towards goals" —*Keith Davis*
- "Leadership is the ability of a manager to induce subordinates (followers) to work with confidence and zeal". —*Koontz and O'Donnell*
- "Leadership is the ability to influence a group toward the achievement of goals". —*Robbins*

The above definitions of leadership emphasize that a leader is more than just a manager. The distinction between a leader and a manager is summarized as follows: The manager administers; the leader innovates. The manager is a copy; the leader is an original. The manager maintains control and order; the leader develops. The manager focuses on systems, tasks, structures, and results; the leader focuses on people and processes. The manager relies on control; the leader builds relationships, inspires trust, motivates, and generates commitment. The manager has a short-range view; the leader has a long-range perspective. The manager asks how and why; the leader asks what and why. The manager has his eye on the bottom line; the leader deals with the bottom line and has his eyes on the horizon. The manager accepts and protects status quo; the leader creates an environment for change. The manager does things right; the leader does the right thing.

Leadership Style: Leadership style refers to the distinctive manner peculiar to a leader in execution of his duties and responsibilities. The style depends mainly on the leader's personality and traits developed under a particular cultural background.

Leadership in Islam : Muslims build their behaviour as leader and/or as follower upon the word of God as revealed in their Holy Book, the Quran. They believe that the Prophet Mohamed (Sal) has modeled the way for Muslim leaders and followers for all times. This belief is supported when God says the following about Mohamed (Sal) *"And you stand an exalted standard of character"* (Quran 68:4). Mohamed's (Sal) example, then, is what both Muslim leaders and followers seek to emulate. According to Prophet Mohamed (Sal), leadership in Islam is not reserved for small elite. Rather, depending upon the situation, every person is the "shepherd" of a flock, and occupies a position of leadership. He added, *"Each of you is a guardian, and each of you will be asked about his subjects"* (Bhukari). In most circumstances in life, Muslims are urged to appoint a leader and follow him. According to Prophet Mohamed (Sal) Muslims must appoint a leader during a trip, select a leader to lead the prayer and choose a leader for other group activities. Leadership then can be depicted as a process by which the leader seeks the voluntary participation of followers in an effort to reach certain objectives. This definition suggests that leadership is essentially a process whereby the leader guides the willing followers. At all times a leader must remember that he cannot compel others to do things against their will. *"Let there be no compulsion in religion"* (Quran 2:256). Islamic Leadership style includes consensus-building traits such as *Shura* and it is unlike authoritative leadership where the leader is the center of all authority and unlike the loose *laissez-faire* style where the group with no direction or supervision and guidance makes all of its own decision. Rather it is a unique style.

Shura : *Shura* is the Islamic process of consultation among those with knowledge of the issues involved and is best accomplished by discussion among those most aware of the situation before deciding upon any issue. Four cardinal Islamic values, namely, personal freedom, justice, equality and human dignity are conceived within the *Shura* framework of administration. *Shura* is the process and order in Islam by which, the leader consults with his members and hears their opinion before deciding upon any issue. The Quran emphatically orders the Prophet to consult, through the following verse: *"So pardon them and ask forgiveness for them and consult with them upon the conduct of affairs"* (Quran 3:159).

Islamic Culture and its value structure: Islam is an Arabic word. It is derived from two root-words: One *Salm,* meaning peace and the other *Silm* meaning submission. Islam stands for "a commitment to surrender one's will to the Will of God" and thus to be at peace with the Creator and with all that has been created by Him. Religious and secular are not two autonomous categories; they represent two sides of the same coin. (Maududi).

Culture is a system of shared values and beliefs that produce norms of behaviour. Islamic culture comprises the following: (1) belief in one God, (2) belief in the hereafter and reward and punishment, (3) independence, (4) responsibility and accountability, (5) participation, (6) justice and equity, (7) trust, dignity and privacy, (8) cost and time efficiency, (9) caring and sharing, and (10) mercy towards humans, animals and the environment.

Rashid Moten points out in his article, 'Islamization of knowledge', that Western social science confuses or conceals normative consideration; Islam states its values explicitly. The Stockholm Seminar of 1981 on "Knowledge and Values" identified ten concepts which generate the basic values of an Islamic culture; *tawhid* (unity), *khilafah* (vicegerency), *ibadah* (worship), *ilm* (knowledge), *halal* (permissible), *haram* (prohibited), *adl* (justice), *zulm* (tyranny), *istislah* (public interest) and *dhiya* (waste).

Tawhid (Unity)

The essential comprehensive characteristic of Islam and its primary basis is *tawhid*, the unity of Allah, which affirms the radical monotheism of Islam. Allah is One, He has no partner and there is none worthy of worship except him. *Tawhid* extends to all of creation and thus signifies unity of Allah, the unity of the community of the faithful, the unity of life as a totality, and the unity of the temporal and spiritual. *Tawhid* provides one, single direction and guarantees a unified spirit for its adherents. It perfects the ethical consciousness of mankind and enters humanity with the hidden power of "wisdom", which nurtures and perfects it.

Khilafah (Vicegerency)

A corollary of *tawhid* is *khilafah*, mankind's vicegerency of Allah. As a vicegerent, mankind is not free but responsible and accountable to Allah. One's vocation and destiny, therefore, is the service of Allah, or fulfilment of Divine Will. Allah has "*not created Mankind and Jinn but to serve him.*" (Quran 51:56). The *khilafah* consists of the fulfilment of the responsibility of sustaining the self and other creatures in accordance with the will of Allah. The faithful execution of this sublime responsibility is, in fact, the true nature of *ibadah* (worship or service to Allah).

Ibadah (Worship)

The concept of worship, *ibadah,* is very wide in Islam. It does not mean merely ritual or specific form of prayer, but a life of continuous prayer and unremitting obedience to Allah. *Ibadah* encompasses all activities of life—spiritual, social, economic, and political—provided they are in accordance with the rules as laid down and if their ultimate objective is to seek the pleasure of Allah. As a *Khalifah,* man's activities may be grouped under two headings: *haqq Allah,* i.e., duties and obligations due directly to Allah, and *haqq al-ibad,* duties to oneself, to fellow beings and to other creatures for the pleasure of Allah.

Ilm (knowledge)

Among the many manifestations of *ibadah* and a pre-requisite to its effective performance is *ilm,* knowledge. In its totality the concept of *ilm* in Islam is very vast. It ranges in its meaning from the Sufi understanding of the term *marifah* (gnosis) to the interpretation of knowledge as it concerns every day activities of the individual. *Ilm,* in general, is divided into two categories: revealed knowledge, which basically includes the *Quran* and the *Sunnah,* and science-derived knowledge, which is acquired through experience, observation and research. The former category is further sub-divided into *fard al-ayn,* which is binding on every individual Muslim, and *fard al-kifayah,* which is binding on the community as a whole but which some members of the community can discharge on its behalf.

Ilm is mentioned in the Quran with unusual frequency and has been paired, in verse 30:56, with *iman* (faith), which, according to verse 3:71, follows upon *haqq* (truth). The pursuit of ilm, according to a Hadith, is incumbent upon every Muslim even if it entails traveling far of China. However, *ilm* becomes a value only if it is pursued within the value-framework of Islam. Unlike the Western hackneyed phrase of "knowledge for knowledge sake" or that entire convoluted argument that "all knowledge is good," Islam considers *ilm* as a value and an act of *ibadah* only when it is pursued for the benefit of the individual or the community and ultimately for gaining the pleasure of Allah.

Halal (permissible), adl (justice), istislah (public interest)

In Islam, *ilm* has to be value-based and must have a function and a purpose. In other words, knowledge is not for its own sake but serve as a way to salvation, and not all kinds of knowledge would serve the purpose. Consequently, Muslim scholars throughout history have occupied themselves in sifting out the kind of *ilm*, which is Islamically sanctioned. This lead to the categorization of knowledge into *halal* and *haram,* permitted and prohibited or the praiseworthy and blameworthy. *Halal* includes all knowledge and activity that is beneficial for an individual, society and the environment. An *ilm,* which is *halal,* seeks to promote *adl,* social justice, and *istislah,* public interest. *Adl* in its multidisciplinary facets, and *istislah,* with its wider dimension, ensure that knowledge is pursued to promote universal equity, individual freedom, social dignity, and values that enhance the well-being of Muslim society and culture.

Haram (prohibited), zulm (tyranny), dhiya (waste)

Haram or blameworthy research includes all that is destructive for man and his environment in its physical, intellectual, and spiritual sense. Research promoting alienation, dehumanization, environmental destruction, and others, which are *per se* evil, are, therefore rejected. These activities are tyrannical, or *zulm,* and are categorized as *dhiya,* wastage. Even astrology, which is part of knowledge, falls under this category. Its practice was declared unlawful by the Prophet (Sal), since the evil in it is greater than the good it contains. Mankind as the best of Allah's creation is endowed with conscience, wisdom, and discretion and is inspired to strive together toward all that is good, to eradicate tyranny, and to establish justice and faith in Allah (Quran 2:148, 193).

It should be evident that the matrices of values outlined above are organically related to each other, and impart a unique character to the epistemology of Islam. The discipline of social science that emerges following such a strategy is able to rank a variety of human ends by reference to an overall sense of what is important and what is good in general. It introduces a principle of coherence into otherwise incoherent human sciences; it reflects upon what is important and meaningful in human life. It thus offers a basis for discriminating between what is relevant and irrelevant, significant and insignificant, virtuous and vicious.

SOURCES OF STUDY

The main sources of the present study are listed as below:

1. Original Sources

(a) *Quran*: The final book or revelation from Allah to mankind, revealed to the Prophet Mohamed (Sal) over a span of 23 years. Believing in revelation, its purity and its perfection induce us to consider it as the major source of knowledge. The Quran, the primary source of Islamic Law (Shariyah) is used extensively throughout this research. References to Quranic verses appear as, for example (Quran 3:159) meaning chapter 3 and verse 159. Quranic citations in this study are mostly from "The Holy Quran's English translation of the meanings and commentary by Abdullah Yusuf Ali" and from the meaning of the Glorious Quran, Text and Explanatory Translation by Mohamed M. Pickthall are also referred.

(b) *Hadith or Sunnah*: Every utterance of the Prophet Mohamed (Sal) apart from the Quran, and his every deed from the beginning of his mission to the last moment of his life, constitute his Sunnah. In references to Hadith or Sunnah, the name of the book or compiler is given after each citation.

2. Documents and Manuscripts

Documents of early Islamic history related to the life of Prophet Mohamed (Sal); rightly guided Caliphs and the Companions were studied for the purpose of analyzing leadership traits, qualities and ethics. Few Arabic manuscripts and articles were got translated and referred.

3. Other Materials

Relevant contemporary literature in the form of books, journals, articles, reports and documents were of vital use for this study.

4. Consultation with Scholars

The study has greatly benefited by the sound Islamic background and rich subject expertise of the researcher's Guide & Supervisor. Other Islamic scholars and subject experts were also consulted and valuable information related to the topic under study was collected.

5. Personal Experience

Finally, the researcher, who himself is a Muslim and has been in the profession of teaching Management subject over two decades, can claim a wider perspective that enables him to make sound judgment in the area of his study.

METHODOLOGY

The contemporary literature of the social sciences reflects many research approaches. Some of which are: (a) exploratory or formulative, (b) descriptive, (c) analytic, (d) diagnostic, (e) experimental, and (f) comparative. The researcher had adopted mainly the exploratory or formulative approach, in studying "Leadership style and Shura system in Islamic culture". However, descriptive, analytic and comparative methods are also used.

It is believed that empiricism, as a basis of research cannot be relied in the field of understanding and formulating human behaviour. The conclusions based on empiricism are generally not universal and are more applicable to the societies in which the experiments had been carried out. In this study, empirical approach was not adopted due to the following facts. The contributions of contemporary management are so numerous; many of its conclusions were derived from empirical studies that were carried out within a certain group selected on certain basis. Western empirical social science is based upon the assumption that human behaviour is patterned and that these regularities can be scientifically investigated and expressed as generalizations that approximate the universality of scientific law or theory in the physical sciences. But numerous studies in the field have explained the social scientist's inevitable bias as emanating from personality subjective factors. The sociologist or the psychologist, according to this view, can't entirely liberate himself from individual inclinations, values and interests in going about studying the phenomena, which belong to each field.

Total objectivity in the sciences of man and society is beyond human reach according to the German sociologist, Max Weber. Religious spiritual beliefs and culture values are real components of the human makeup and their impact on human behaviour is real as well. Rigid empirico-positivist and behavioural frameworks are short-sighted approaches in their perspectives distinct human factors as active forces on the individual's behaviour, scientific credibility of their explanation of man's behaviour could only remain shallow and distorted.

The differences in society induce variations in the leadership style. Moreover, some of the contemporary managerial concepts are based on certain premises of thought that are strictly contradictory to the teachings of Islam and are, for that matter, limited, and they are often controversial among the Western scholars as well. It is common knowledge that, only the Creator (the Almighty God) is perfect and knowledgeable in all respects. So studies and methodology on the basis of His commandments (Quran and Hadith), which are considered as original sources of knowledge, will provide perfect and additional knowledge to the field of leadership styles.

CHAPTERISATION

The Study has been presented in the form of a Thesis with the Chapters arranged as follows:

Chapter – I : Introduction

This chapter explains the moral dimensions of the topic under research, which forms the background of the study, outlines the statement of the problem, sets out the objectives, defines the terms used, indicates the sources and presents the research methodology.

Chapter – II : Review of literature

This chapter illustrates a brief overview of the research done on leadership in management science. Various Western theories of leadership are also reviewed.

Chapter – III : Theoretical framework : Leadership traits and organisational chemistry in Islamic perspective

This chapter describes the personal qualities of a successful leader. Eleven sets of important traits are identified. Each trait is explained with references from the Holy Quran and incidents from the life history of Prophet Mohamed (Sal) and his companions. Organisational chemistry is the articulation of leadership traits with various functions such as direction, mobilisation and integration, performed by a leader while executing the leadership task. The leader's role as a follower is also enlightened in this chapter.

Chapter – IV : Shura (mutual consultation) system

This chapter deals with the *Shura* (mutual consultation) system. It is one of the cardinal principles of leadership under Islamic culture. The various aspects of *Shura* such as, significance of *Shura,* factors required for the fulfilment of *Shura;* *Shura* and democracy; *Shura* and Autocratic style of leadership; *Shura* and decision-making; different forms of consultation; organisation of *Shura* council and its functions; the leader and the council are articulated elaborately in this chapter.

Chapter – V : Islamic theory of leadership : Unique features

This chapter enlightens the core part of the research. The psychological underpinning of the behavioural aspects of the leader and followers are analysed and on the basis of the divine guidance, an Islamic theory of leadership is formulated and furnished. Based on this, the unique features of a Muslim leadership style are also explained in this chapter.

Chapter — VI : Summary and Conclusion

This last chapter presents the chapter-wise summary of the entire study. The major findings and overall conclusion are also reported in this chapter.

References

Al-Buraey, Muhammad (1985), Management and Administration in Islam, By Kegan Paul Interntional Ltd., UK, p. 348.

Beekun, Rafik and Jamal Badawi (1999), Leadership Process in Islam, Islamic Training Foundation, USA.

Beekun, Rafik and Jamal Badawi (1999), Leadership : An Islamic Perspective, Amana Publications, Maryland, USA.

Davis, K. (1980), Human Behaviour at Work: Organizational Behaviour, Tata McGraw-Hill Publishing Co. Ltd., New Delhi.

Eldersveld, S.J., *et. al.*, (1961), Research in Political Behaviour, in S. Sidney Ulmer, ed., Introductory Reading in Political Behaviour, Chicago: Rand McNally & Co.

George O. Terry (1977), Principles of Management, Richard D. Irwin, Homewood, 1977.

Hart, Michael (1979), The 100: Ranking of the Most Influential Persons in History, Golden Book Center, p. 33.

Hemant Kumar Sabat (1998), New Era of Leadership, Indian Management, July, p. 81.

Jabnoun, Naceur (2001), Islam and Management, International Islamic Publishing House, Riyadh, Saudi Arabia.

Koontz, Harold, and O'Donnell, Cyril (1972), Principles of Management: An analysis of Managerial Functions, McGraw Hill Book Company Inc., Tokyo, 1972.

Linda Smircich (1983), Concept of Organisational Analysis, *Administrative Science Quarterly*, Sept., p. 342.

Mahmoud Dhaouadi (1990), A Critical assessment of the Issues of Objectivity and Subjectivity in Contemporary Western Socio-Behavioural Thought and its Muslim Khaldunian Counterpart, *The American Journal of Islamic Social Sciences*, Vol. 7, No. 2, p. 201.

Maudoodi, Sayyid, Abu A'la (1991), The Islamic Movement: Dynamics of Values, Power and Change, The Islamic Foundation, U.K.

Maudoodi, Sayyid Abul A'la (2000), Towards Understanding Islam, Markazi Maktaba Islami Publishers, New Delhi, p. 10.

Moten, Rashid (1989), Islamization of Knowledge: Methodology of Research in Political Science, *The American Journal of Islamic Social Sciences*, Vol. 7, No. 2, 1990, pp. 162-64.

Muqim, Mohammad (Editor) (1994), Research Methodology in Islamic Perspective, Institute of Objective Studies, New Delhi.

Parukh, S.K. (1995), The leadership conundrum, Indian Management, October, p. 39.

Qutb, Muhammad (1982), Islam the Misunderstood Religion, Markazi Maktaba Islami, Delhi.

Ritz, G. (1984), Sociological Theory, New York: Alfred Knopf, pp. 121-57.

Robbins, S.P. (1979), Organizational Behaviour: Concepts and Controversies, Englewood Cliffs, New Jersey, Prentice-Hall, Inc., p. 240.

Sadek Jawad Sulaiman (1999), The Shura Principle in Islam, Al-Hawar Center, Inc.

Schriescheim, C.A., Tolliver, J.M., and Behling, O.C. (1978), Leadership Theory: Some Implications for Managers, MSU Topics, (26): 35.

Tannenbaum (1961), Leadership and Organization, McGraw-Hill, New York.

Weber, M. (1949), The Methodology of Social Sciences, Chicago: Free Press.

Quranic References

(21:73), (3:159), (21:107), (68:4), (2:256), (30:56), (3:71), (2:148) and (2:193).

2

Studies on Leadership

This study aims at the articulation of a universally acceptable theory of leadership in the light of revealed knowledge. Hence, an evaluation and critical appraisal of the existing theories is considered necessary. This chapter attempts to furnish a concise outline on leadership from the Trait Approach to Constructive Developmental Theory and the review of literature on leadership in different culture. The names of the authors whose writings have been reviewed are presented at the end of the chapter to facilitate readability.

The issue of leadership can be traced back to the origin of mankind. A considerable move towards the systematic study of leadership was done during the nineteenth century. Carlyle's (1841) discussion of heroic leadership and Galton's (1870) emphasis on the inheritance of leadership qualities were influential at this time. Weber (1947) distinguished three bases upon which a leader's authority might rest. These he identified as:

1. *Rational grounds*: resting on a belief in the legality of patterns of normative rules and the right of those elevated to authority under such rules to issue commands (legal authority).

2. *Traditional grounds*: resting on an established belief in the sanctity of immemorial traditions and the legitimacy of the states of those exercising authority under them (traditional authority).
3. *Charismatic grounds*: resting on devotion to specific and exceptional sanctity, heroism or exemplary character of an individual person, and of the normative patterns or order revealed or ordained by him (charismatic authority).

Scholars from the USA made an attempt to specify different styles of leadership during 1960s and 1970s and could find mainly two styles, namely, "Task-oriented" and "People-oriented". Stogdill (1974) lamented the general trend in the literature to believe that, "all forms of people-oriented behaviour are identical in character and all forms of task-oriented behaviour are merely variants of authoritarian.

Recognizing the importance of the human element in organisations, behavioural scientists have conducted extensive research to find out what makes a leader effective, whether, it is the personality of the leader or his behaviour, or the type of followers he has, or the situation in which he works, or a combination of all these. They have failed to give one satisfactory answer. They have developed different theories or approaches to leadership. These theories may be reviewed hereunder.

TRAIT APPROACH TO LEADERSHIP

Trait theory is based on the belief that a person who possesses exceptional traits or qualities of excellence becomes the leader of the group. This theory, which is the earliest one, seeks to determine the universal personal traits of effective leaders. In 1930s studies were conducted to isolate leadership traits. A number of traits were identified by a number of researchers. The term trait can refer to a number of individual attributes that can also include personality values, needs and motives. Traits like, morality, responsibility, intelligence, ability, sociality, emotional balance, communication, knowledge, creativity, tact, diplomacy, objectivity, self-confidence, risk taking, independence, perfection, judgment, task orientation, assertiveness, administration, enthusiastic, humane, imaginative, decisive, and so on.

Terman (1904) conducted the first known study on the trait theory. He asked teachers to describe the playground leaders. They were reported to be active, quick, and skilful in devising and playing games and good looking. In addition, boy leaders were said to be stronger and brighter, where as, girl leaders were said to be of good disposition and temper. The numerous later studies, which used not only the reputation of leaders, but also self-reports and ability tests as these were developed, have been frequently reviewed. Stogdill (1948) located 104 studies while Mann (1959) located about 75. Later commentators such as Stogdill (1974) Yukl (1981) and Bryman (1986) have all noted the substantial effect of the earlier reviews upon later conceptualization of the leadership process. Both the Mann and the Stogdill reviews concluded that personality variables account for only a minor proportion of variance in leadership behaviour. As Stogdill (1948) put it, "A person does not become a leader by virtue of the possession of some combination of traits, but the pattern of personal characteristics of the leader must bear some relevant relationship to the characteristics, activities, and goals of the followers". Mann conducted his review by computing more than 1400 median correlations between leadership and each of the variable studied. The highest relationship found was a median correlation of 0.25 between leadership and intelligence. Lord de Vader and Alliger (1986) have attempted to update the validity of Mann's conclusions, both by re-examining the studies he reviewed and adding other more recent ones. They found within Mann's sample only 19 studies, which gave sufficient statistical detail for further analysis. This led to an estimate of the correction between intelligence and leadership of 0.52, compared to Mann's estimate of 0.25.

Kenny and Zacarro (1983) reanalysed data from a previous study in which Barnlund (1962) had concluded that task situation, not traits, determined leader emergence in laboratory experimental groups. The reanalysis indicated that 49 to 82 percent of the variance in leader emergence was due to some stable characteristics of the person. Thus the most recent view is that, intelligence and possibly other personal qualities do play a vital role in the emergence of leaders in unstructured settings.

Stogdill (1974) again conducted a survey of series of 163 studies linking personality and leadership. He includes indiscriminately, studies, which assessed the leader's effectiveness, and those, which assessed leader's emergence. He concludes that the earlier reviews had underestimated the role of personality in effective leadership, and that personality must be considered as one among many factors, which contributes to leadership. Stogdill's ideal profile for successful leaders was, "The leader is characterised by a strong drive for responsibility and task completion vigour and persistence in pursuit of goals. Originality in problem-solving drive to exercise initiative in social situations, self-confidence and sense of personal identity, willingness to accept consequences of decision and action, readiness to absorb interpersonal stress, willingness to tolerate frustration and delay, ability to influence other persons behaviour and capacity to structure social interaction system to the purpose at hand".

Davis (1972) identified four factors, which according to him were important for a successful leader. They were: (1) intelligence, (2) social maturity, (3) inner motivation, and (4) achievement drive and human relations attitude. Kirkpatrick and Hoke (1991) said that there were six traits by which leaders are distinguished from non-leaders: (1) ambition and energy, (2) the desire to lead, (3) honesty and integrity, (4) self-confidence, (5) intelligence, and (6) job-relevant knowledge.

In spite of this relative success Yukl and Van Fleet (1982) say that though some traits increase the likelihood of successful leadership, none of them guarantee the leader/manager of it. The main reason for the failure of the trait theory was that it did not take into accounts the needs and expectations of the followers nor did it accord any consideration to situational factor. The theories did not explain how the traits of the leader could affect delayed outcome like the performance of the group. The typical behavioural outcomes of the traits were not generalised. In addition, the cause and effect were not distinguished in the theories—whether, the traits make a person leader or the leadership generates the traits in the person.

Another reason is that the research has weighed all the traits equally, without making clear the relative importance or unimportance of each. Due to the above reasons the researchers preferred the study of attitude or behaviour of the leaders instead of traits.

BEHAVIOURAL APPROACH TO LEADERSHIP

This approach was initiated in the year 1930 by the energies of Kurt Lewin. In this view there are specifiable sets of behaviours, which we may delineate as the skills of leadership, but they are not inherent in the person. Indeed once identified, the skills may be taught to others, who may thereby become effective leaders. The classic study in this tradition was that by Lewin, Lippit and White (1939), who examined the impact of the different leadership styles upon boy's Clubs. By using three club leaders, each of whom role-played each leader style in turn, the effect of personality upon the results was essentially eliminated. The researchers' decision to compare autocratic and democratic styles of leadership was an expression of their preoccupation with the political events of the late thirties. The impact of the study shows, how widely shared was those preoccupations. The main period of the behavioural approaches to leadership occurred between 1945, with the Ohio State and Michigan studies and mid-1960s with the development of Managerial Grid.

Ohio State Leadership Studies

The leadership studies initiated in 1945 by the Bureau of Business Research at Ohio State University attempted to identify various dimensions of leader behaviours. The staff defining leadership as the behaviours of an individual when directing the activities of a group toward a goal attainment, eventually narrowed the description of leader behaviour to two dimensions: initiating structure and consideration. Initiating structure refers to "the leader's behaviour in delineating the relationship between himself and member of the work group and in endeavoring to establish well-defined pattern of organization, channels of communication, and methods of procedure". On the other hand, consideration refers to "behaviour indicative of friendship, mutual trust, respect, and warmth in the members of his staff".

The Ohio state staff developed the Leader Behaviour Description Questionnaire (LBDQ), an instrument designed to describe how leaders carry out their activities. The LBDQ contains fifteen items pertaining to Consideration and an equal number for Initiating Structure. Although the major emphasis in the Ohio State Leadership studies was on observed behaviour, the staff did develop the Leader Opinion Questionnaire (LOQ) to gather data about the self-perceptions that leaders have about their own leadership style. Leader(s), subordinate(s), superior(s), or associate(s) (peers) completed the LBDQ, but the leaders themselves scored the LOQ. It was during these studies that leader behaviour was first plotted on two separate axes rather than on a single continuum. The LBDQ has been used in a number of studies in its original and modified form.

Group Dynamic Studies

Dorwin Cartwright and Alvin Zander, summarizing the findings of numerous studies at the Research cCenter for Group Dynamics, claim that group objectives fall into one of two categories: (1) the achievement of some specific group goal or (2) the maintenance or strengthening of the group itself. According to Cartwright and Zander, the type of behaviour involved in goal achievement is illustrated by these examples: the manager "initiates action, keeps members' attention on the goal, clarifies the issue and develops a procedural plan". On the other hand, characteristic behaviours for group maintenance are the manager "keeps interpersonal relations pleasant, arbitrates dispute, provides encouragement, gives the minority a chance to be heard, stimulates self-direction and increases the interdependence among members".

Rensis Likert's Management Systems

Using the earlier Michigan studies as a starting place, Rensis Likert (1961) did some extensive research to discover the general pattern of management used by high-producing managers in contrast to that used by the other managers. He found that "supervisors with the best records of performance focus their primary attention on the human aspects of their subordinates' problems and on endeavouring to build effective work groups with high performance goals".

Michigan Leadership Studies

The Researchers at the University of Michigan were engaged in a study to identify the relationship among the leader behaviour, group process and group performance. It was a series of group studies undertaken by the researchers at Michigan University with section managers in an Insurance Company (Katz Macoby and Morse, 1950), supervisors in a manufacturing company (Katz and Khan, 1953) and supervisors in Railroad section gangs (Katz, Macoby *et. al.*, 1951). The studies were conducted through interviews and questionnaires; data on group productivity was collected objectively to clarify the managers as effective and ineffective. These studies identified two types of behaviours; which they called Employee (or) Relationship-oriented and Task (or) Production-oriented.

Leaders, who are described as employee-oriented, stress the relationship aspect of their job. They feel that every employee is important and take interest in everyone, accepting their individuality and personal needs. Task orientation emphasizes production and technical aspects of the job; employees are seen as tools to accomplish the goals of the organization. These two orientations parallel the *authoritarian* (task) and *democratic* (relationship) concept of the leader behaviour continuum.

The implication throughout Likerts writings is that the ideal and most productive leader behaviour for industry is employee-centered or democratic. Yet, his own findings raise questions as to whether there can be an ideal or single normatively good style of leader behaviour that can be applied in all leadership situations.

Evidence suggesting that "a single ideal or normative style of leader behaviour is unrealistic" was provided when a study was done in an industrial setting in Nigeria (Paul Hersey, 1965). The results were almost the exact opposite of Likert's findings. Therefore, based on the definition of leadership process as a function of the leader, the followers, and other situational variables, a single ideal type of leader behaviour seems unrealistic.

Managerial Grid

Robert R. Blake and Jane S. Mouton have popularized their concepts in their Managerial Grid and have used them extensively in organization and management development programs (1964). In the managerial Grid, five different types of leadership-based on concern for production (task) and concern for people (relationship) are located in four quarters similar to those identified by the Ohio State Studies. The five leadership styles are described as follows:

> (1) Impoverished, (2) Country club, (3) Task, (4) Middle-of-the Road, and (5) Team (Robert Blake 1964). The Managerial Grid tends to be attitudinal model that measures the values and feelings of a manager.

Reddin (1967) took the managerial grid as the platform and developed a three-dimensional model of leadership. He was the first to introduce the concept of effectiveness. He suggested that all the four leadership styles of the grid would be effective depending on the situation. He identified eight styles of leadership under two categories; namely, effective and ineffective:

> The Effective Styles were: (1) The Executive, (2) The Developer, (3) The Benevolent-Autocrat, and (4) The Bureaucrat.
> *The Ineffective Styles were*: (1) The Compromiser, (2) The Missionary, (3) The Autocrat, and (4) The Deserter.

While some researchers such as Blake, Mouton and McGregor have argued that there is "one best" style of leadership—a style that maximizes productivity and satisfaction, and growth and development in all situations, further research in the last several decades has clearly supported the contention that there is no one best leadership style (Bennis, 1976). Successful and effective leaders are able to adapt their style to fit the requirements of the situation. To amplify their idea, it is necessary to place the current state of leadership theory and Situational Leadership, in particular into perspective.

SITUATIONAL APPROACH TO LEADERSHIP

The contribution of a leader's actions to the effectiveness of his organization cannot be determined without considering the nature of the situation in which that behaviour is displayed.

There are three main components of the leadership process: the *leader*, the *follower*, and the *situation*. Situational approach to leadership examines the interplay among their variables in order to find causal relationships that lead to predictability of behaviour. While there are many situational models and theories we will focus on five that have received wide attention in leadership research:

Tannenbaum-Schmidt Continuum of Leader Behaviour

The article published in *Harvard Business Review* (1973), (original article published in 1957) by Robert Tannenbaum and Warren H. Schmidt, titled "How to choose a Leadership Pattern" was considered one of the most significant situational approaches to leadership. This approach was named, "Tannenbaum-Schmidt Continuum of Leader Behaviour".

Here, a leader selects one out of seven possible leader behaviours depending upon the forces among the leader, follower and the situation.

Tannenbaum and Schmidt depicted a broad range of styles (behaviour) as a continuum moving from authoritarian or boss-centered or task-oriented behaviour at one end to democratic or subordinate-centered leader behaviour at the other end.

Often this continuum is extended beyond democratic leader behaviour to include a *laissez-faire* style that permits the group members to do whatever they want to do. It is interesting to note that in the 1973 reprint of their article in the *Harvard Business Review,* Tannenbaum and Schmidt commented that interrelationship among leader, follower and situation were becoming increasingly complex.

Fiedlers Contingency Theory and LPC Research

Fred Fiedler was widely respected as the Father of the Contingency Model. The Contingency Theory of leadership is built around the Least Preferred Coworker (LPC) measure of leader personality. Its basic premise is that a leader's description

Fig. I
Continuum of Leader Behaviour

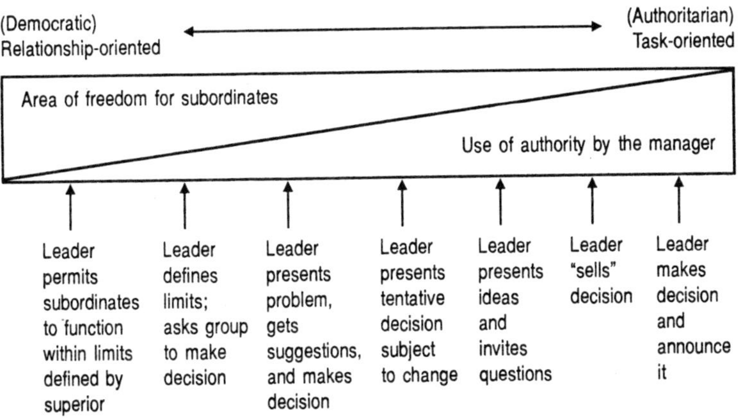

Source : Heresy, P. and K.H. Blanchard (1982), Management of Organizational Behaviour.

of the person with whom he or she had the greatest difficulty working reflects a basic leadership style. Fiedler's model distinguishes high LPC leaders, whom he initially considered to be task-oriented from low LPC leaders whom he desecrated as relationship-oriented. He suggests that three major situational variables seems to determine whether a given situation is favourable to leaders: (1) their personal relations with the members of their group (leader-member relations), (2) the degree of structure in the task that their group has been assigned to perform (task structure), and (3) the power and authority that their position provides (position power).

Leader-member relations refer to the degree of confidence and respect the subordinates have in the leader. The better the relationship between the leader and subordinates the easier it will be for the leader to exercise influence. Task structure implies whether the task of subordinate is routine or complex. More structured is the task greater the influence the leader can exercise. Leader position, power refer to the ability of the leader to influence the behaviour of the subordinates through legitimate power.

These three variables determine whether a given situation is favourable or unfavourable to a leader. The favourableness of a situation is the degree to which the situation enables the leader to exercise influence over the group. The recommended leadership style varies with the situation.

House-Mitchell Path-Goal Theory

According to this theory, leaders are effective because of their inspect on subordinates' motivation, ability to perform effectively and satisfactions. The theory is called Path-Goal because its major concern is how the leader influences the subordinates' perceptions of their work goals, personal goals and paths to goal attainment. The theory suggests that a leader's behaviour is motivating or satisfying to the degree that the behaviour increases subordinate goals attainment and clarifies the paths to these goals.

Leaders do this best according to Path-Goal Theory when they supply what is missing from the situation. For example, in an unstructured task situation, leader may increase job

FIG. 2

Hypothetical Relationships between Directive Leadership and Subordinate Satisfaction with Task Structure as a Contingency Factor

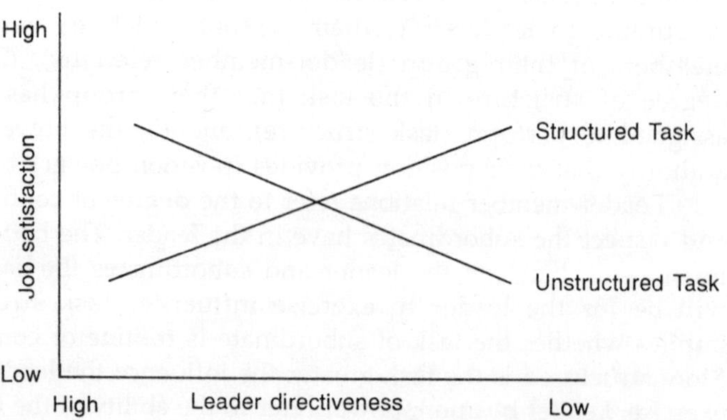

Source : Heresy, P. and K.H. Blanchard (1982), Management of Organizational Behaviour.

satisfaction by supplying leader directiveness. Job satisfaction is high in a situation that is unstructured—for example, in a basic research lab, job satisfaction would be highest when leader directiveness is high; job satisfaction would be low if leader directiveness is low. In a structured task situation—for example, in an assembly line, job satisfaction would be highest when leader directiveness is low and job satisfaction would be lowest when leader directiveness is high. Leadership behaviour should help reduce the frustration and mitigate the dissatisfying nature of highly structured tasks. Further it is announced that if follower's tasks are highly structured, the required activities are clear to followers and leader task behaviour (providing deviation and institution) is less important. If followers are performing relatively unstructured tasks, the Path-Goal theory proposes that a leadership style high on task behaviour and low on relationship behaviour will be the most effective.

Vroom-Yetton Contingency Model

Victor Vroom and Phillip Yetton (1973) presented a model of leadership, which focuses on leadership acts in settings, which require an explicit decision. They explore the criteria that can be used to determine whether and how the leader should involve subordinates in certain kinds of decision situation. Five main types of leader styles are distinguished, each with several variants and seven types of environmental contingency. In the original model, these are arrived at, through a series of binary choices. Leadership is classified as autocratic, consultative or based on group decision-making. Both the autocratic and consultative styles are sub-divided into further categories. The decision environment is sub-divided in terms of whether it is important to obtain the highest possible quality decision and whether it is important that others accept the decision once it is made. Where quality is important, three further choices are to be made depending on availability of information, subordinates' acceptance of organizational goals and how structured the problem is.

The importance of this model is that it makes rather precise predictions as to the most effective decision style in a given setting. Vroom and Jago (1978) asked 96 managers to recall successful and unsuccessful decision made by them earlier. It was found that where the managers had done as the model prescribes, 68 percent of decisions had been successful. Where they had not, only 22 percent were successful. Since the managers were unfamiliar with the Vroom-Yetton model, this is impressive.

Hersey-Blanchard Tri-Dimensional Leader Effectiveness Model

Paul Hersey and Kenneth H. Blanchard developed this model in their research efforts. The term task behaviour and relationship behaviour are used to describe concepts similar to consideration and initiating structure of the Ohio state studies. The four basic leader behaviour Quadrants are labeled; high task and low relationship; high task and high relationship; high relationship and low task; and low relationship and low task. (Figure 3).

FIG. 3
Basic Leader Behaviour Style

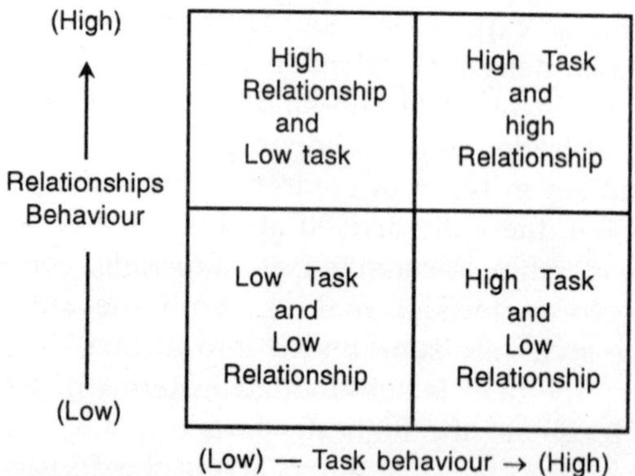

Source : Heresy, P. and K.H. Blanchard (1982), Management of Organizational Behaviour.

These four basic styles depict essentially different leadership styles. The leadership style of an individual is the behaviour pattern that person exhibits, when attempting to influence the activities of others as perceived by those others. This may be very different from the leader's perception of leadership behaviour, which we shall define as self-perception rather than style. A person's leadership style involves some combination of task behaviour and relationship behaviour. The two types of behaviour, 'task' and 'relationship'—which are defined as follows:

Task behaviour—The extent to which leaders are likely to organize and define the roles of the members of their group (followers); to explain what activities each is to do and when, where and how tasks are to be accomplished; char cterised by endeavoring to establish well-defined patterns of organization, channels of communication, and ways of getting jobs accompanied.

Relationship behaviour—The extent to which leaders are likely to maintain personal relationship between themselves and members of their group (followers) by opening up channels of communication, providing socio-emotional support, "psychological strokes", and facilitating behaviours.

The Power Influence Theory of Leadership

Power generally refers to the capacity of a person to influence a target person. Various researchers have defined it in various ways though the core of all these is the ability to influence (Grimes, 1978, Kotter, 1985, Mintzberg, 1983). Bass (1960) and Etizioni (1961) proposed the most widest—accepted taxonomy of power, position power and personal power. Yukle (1981) proposed a model of power and influence that determined the amount of influence a manager has with his subordinates, peers and superiors. The traits and power of the leader lead to influence behaviour that results in one of the three influence outcomes, commitment, compliance or resistance. Situational variables act as moderators between the influence outcomes and the final performance outcomes of the group.

On the line of this power-influence, research studies influence as a reciprocal process between leader and followers. A theory of leadership that examines the reciprocal influence between the leader and the individual subordinates is the Leader-Member Exchange Theory (LMX) (Dansereau, Graen and Haga) (1975). The theory decides how leaders develop different exchange relationship with subordinates. It proposed that leader behaviour towards the subordinates is not uniform.

Some, who fall in the "in-group" as categorized by the leader early on in the interaction (Liden and Graen, 1980, Liden, Wayne and Still Well, 1993) are trusted, given the leader's time and attention and also special privileges. The basis of classification by the leader is unclear from the theory itself. The general research points out that the "in-group" constituents have personal characteristics similar to the leader, and are more competent and dependable than "out group" members (Kin and Organ, 1982, Duchon, Graen, 1986, Liden Wayne and Still Well, 1993). This classification of the subordinates into in and out-group by the leaders is stable over time according to Liden *et. al.* (1993).

ATTRIBUTION THEORY

An intermediate theory between the contingency and the recent leadership research is the Attribution theory. The Attribution theory in relation to perception has been used to explain the perception of leadership. The theory says the leadership is just an attribution that people make about a person. Using this framework, researchers have proposed that leaders are those persons who are perceived to be intelligent, strong, aggressive, understanding, industrious and so on (Lord-De Vader, and Alliger, 1986) these being the traits. Similarly, from behaviour and contingency theories, a high-high leader (highly oriented towards both the task and the people) is perceived to be effective and in consistent with the attribution of an effective leader and this is regardless of the situation (Powell and Butterfield, 1984).

Another finding of this theory is that rather than day-to-day management or crisis, any extremity in performance, either positive or negative is attributed to the leader (Meindl, Ehrich and Dukerich, 1985). A feature of this theory is that leaders are perceived to be steadfast and committed when they are inflexible (Loel, 1992). Again a leader is perceived to be heroic if he takes up an unpopular cause in the face of opposition and makes a success of it (Staw and Ross, 1980).

TRANSACTIONAL AND TRANSFORMATIONAL THEORY

Burns (1978) identified two types of leadership–transactional and transformational. Transactional leadership occurs when one person takes the initiative in making contact with others for the purpose of an exchange of something valued; that is, "leaders approach followers with an eye towards exchanging" (Burns, 1978). Transformational leadership is based on more than the compliance of followers. It involves shift in the beliefs, needs, and values of followers. According to Burns, "the result of transforming leadership is a relationship of mutual stimulation and elevation may convert leaders into moral agents" (Burns, 1978).

Transformational leadership occurs when leaders and followers raise one another to higher levels of motivation. Transformational leaders motivate followers to work for transcendental goals and self-actualising needs instead of working through simple exchange relationship. Characteristics such as charisma, inspiration, intellectual stimulation, and individualized considerations distinguish transformational leadership from the other types of leadership (Bass, 1985, Bass, Waldman, Avolio, and Bebb, 1987).

Bass (1985) argued that transactional leaders "mostly consider how to marginally improve and maintain the quantity and quality of performance, how to reduce resistance to particular actions, and how to implement decisions (Bass, 1985). In contrast, transformational leaders "attempt and succeed in raising colleagues, subordinates, clients, or constituencies to a greater awareness about the issues of consequence. This heightening of awareness requires a leader with vision, self-confidence, and inner strength to argue successfully for what he or she sees as right or good, not for what is popular or is acceptable according to established wisdom of the time (Bass, 1985).

Bass (1985) sketched a model suggesting that transformational leadership augments and builds on transactional leadership in contributing to subordinate effort, satisfaction, and perceived leader effectiveness. Transformational leadership would also reduce the inclination to quit the organization on the part of the subordinate.

Transformational Leadership and Outcome Variables

Transformational leadership is significantly positively correlated with perceived effectiveness, satisfaction and extra effort and is significantly negatively correlated to the subordinate's intention to quit. Other studies have also found similar relationship. A transformational leader would be expected to have the qualities of inspirational leadership that involve the arousal and heightening of motivation among followers. Envisioning a desired future state and making followers see that vision attracts commitment, and energises people. Vision gets people to commit voluntarily and completely to something worthwhile. Transformational leaders would also exhibit individualized consideration towards followers giving personal attention to those feel neglected and help each follower get what he or she wants.

CONSTRUCTIVE/DEVELOPMENTAL THEORY (CD THEORY)

CD theory (Kegan, 1982; Kegan and Lahey, 1984, Torbert, 1987) identifies discrete stages that represent different ways of "making meaning" of the world that result in a new way of expressing ideas, feelings, and purposes (Merron, Fisher & Torbert, 1987). The six stages of "perspective taking" proposed by Kegan represent successively broader ways of constructing meaning. Kuhnert and Lewis (1987) have applied CD theory to leadership by describing how the manner in which leaders ascribe meaning to, or impose meaning upon, their experience may help to explain their subsequent understanding and action.

According to CD theory, the 'meaning-making' process incorporates two aspects of experience termed subject and object. Subject refers to the process or structure by which individuals organize (make sense of) their experience; it is the lens through which the world is experienced. In contrast object is the content of the experience that can be integrated by the individual. As one progresses through the six stages: (1) reflexes, (2) impulses, perceptions, (3) needs, interests, wishes, (4) interpersonal mutualit, (5) authorship, identity psychic administration, ideology, and (6) inter-individuality; what was subject becomes object; individuals are able to see and reflect upon the way that they previously organized their experience, rather than being defined by it. The fundamental point in determining how meaning is generated lies in the evolution of subject-object relations because that is where the persons' meanings are generated (Lakey, Soureine, Kegan, Goodman and Felix, 1988).

Although CD theory-holders promise for explaining leader influence and effectiveness the framework proposed by Kuhnert and Lewis (1987) refers from the lack of readily available mechanism for assessing what past life experiences contribute to the development of future leaders.

LITERATURE REVIEW ON LEADERSHIP IN DIFFERENT CULTURES

The most appropriate definition for the concept of culture has been debated extensively (Geertz, 1973). For present purpose we shall define culture as agreed ways of interpreting signs, symbols, artifacts and actions. The meanings of actions as perceived by superiors and subordinates may not always be agreed. This would leave the culture of a setting as embracing all those aspects of that setting, which are consensually defined. National cultures, and the cultures of large organizations, may well prove to embody sub-cultures. Early researchers into the leadership attitudes and actions of managers in different countries (e.g., Haire, Ghiselli and Porter, 1966; Bass and Burger, 1979) necessarily compared the responses of managers to their questionnaires without having any particular theory as to how the results would vary from one country to the next. More recently, the work of Hofstede (1980) has provided a framework for classifying work-related values in different national cultures, which makes our task a good deal easier. Hofstede analysed the questionnaire responses of over 116,000 employees in 67 countries, but there were only enough data to analyse from 40 of these. The questionnaire included several questions about the type of boss, which the respondent currently had and would like to have. Hofstede concluded from his study that it was possible to classify the work-related values of those in his sample along four dimensions. These were termed individualism *versus* collectivism, power distance, uncertainty avoidance, and masculinity *versus* femininity. A complete set transformation of the data and factor analysis enabled him to plot the average of responses from each country on each dimension, thereby facilitating comparisons.

On the individualism scale, USA ranks highest of all the 40 countries. In other words, within Hofstede's sample, US respondent laid greatest stress upon the autonomy of the individual, whereas in other countries comparatively greater emphasis was laid upon the way that the person's identity resides within a collective group or organization. On the power distance scale, USA rated 26th with all the countries below it being West European, with the addition of Canada, Australia and New Zeeland. In these countries therefore a lesser psychological distance is reported between superior and subordinate than elsewhere. On uncertainty avoidance the USA ranked 32. Risk-taking was thus more highly valued than in many countries. On masculinity USA ranked 13. In other words, in the USA there was relatively high emphasis on striving, advancement and success.

Critics have queried some aspects of Hofstede's results. For instance, the employees of a single organization may provide a highly aberrant representation of the values current within a particular country. Furthermore, the findings are based upon responses to attitude questionnaires, which may bear little relation to the actual experience of leaders and followers in a given culture.

We can now examine separately the research findings from other individualistic countries, such as those in Western Europe, and from countries, which are more collectively-oriented. Studies of effective leader styles in Europe have yielded findings, which are as inconsistent as those from North America. For instance, in Britain, Argyle, Gardner and Cioffi (1958) found productivity higher in electrical engineering plants where supervisors were democratic and non-punitive, whereas Cooper (1966) found supervisors rated high on task relevance to be the most effective ones in an oil-processing plant. Bryman *et. al.* (1987) found relationship-oriented supervisors to be most effective on construction sites. Sadler (1970) found that among a sample of over 1500 British industrial managers, the leadership style, which they preferred their own boss to use, was a consultative one. The most extensive data concerning the effect of different leader style in Europe are those collected by Heller and Wilpert (1981). Their data shows that the effective leader style of senior executives depends upon a variety of environmental contingencies, which they then attempt to identify. A related project by the Industrial Democracy in Europe research group compared decision-making in 12 European countries. Environmental contingencies such as differences in legislation were found to expect a large influence upon the manner in which decisions were made, particularly major ones (IDE International Research Group, 1981). Some of the early tests of Fiedler's (1967) contingency theory were carried out in Belgium and Holland. Although the results in the Belgian study were not as Fiedler had expected, due to the potency of the linguistic conflict in that country, they nonetheless made it very plain that different leader style were required in different settings. Results from Israel, which scores at the median of Hofstede's individualism-collectivism scale have also been mixed. Fleishman and Simmons (1970) found those Israeli foremen who were effective scored high on both initiating structure and consideration. However, Mannheim, Rim and Grinberg (1967) reported that both among manual workers and clerical workers, preferred supervisors were those who were high on consideration, without regard to the level of their initiation of structure.

In contrast to these results, studies conducted in collectively-oriented societies have given much more consistent support to theories of leader style which specify two components of effectiveness. The research conducted by Misumi (1985) over 40 years in Japan has shown that effective supervisors in that country are those who score high both in their orientation toward task performance which he terms (P) and in their orientation towards team maintenance (M). This finding has been replicated in coalmines, shipbuilding yards, banks, local government offices, bus companies and many others. Further replications in findings are consistent with Japanese culture in general, not just the work culture. The P and M measures used in Misumi's experiments and surveys are not conceptualized in the same way as the Ohio state measures, but an English translation of the M scale has been found to correlate very highly with consideration items and P scale has components which have some similarity to Production emphasis and Initiating structure measures (Peterson, Maiya and Herreid, 1987; Peterson, Smith and Tayeb 1987).

In a similar manner Bond and Hwang (1986) review studies of leader style undertaken in Taiwan, Translation of the Ohio state leader style measures show positive relations between both consideration and initiating structure and performance, measures in factories, local government offices, and schools. Sinha's (1981, 1984) studies in India support the view that the effective leader can be characterised as a Nurturant Task or NT leader. The two dimensions of NT leader behaviour again appear related to the Ohio state scales. Furthermore, Ayman and Chemers (1983) found both Ohio state leadership scales related to productivity in a factory in Iran, although in this case both scales loaded on a single factor. In Brazil, bank employees reacted positively to supervisors who were considerate but provided close supervision (Farris and Butterfield, 1972). Workers in Peru were found to favour supervisors who emphasized production but were thought to understand the problems of workers (White and Williams, 1963). This last study also explored cultural differences in the manner in which consideration might be expressed.

The series of studies have shown that in all the countries, subordinates who evaluated their current work situation highly also evaluated their supervisor as high on both performance (P) and Maintenance (M), just as Misumi's (1985) theory predicts. Western researchers might well argue that such a concordance of the various different ratings by the subordinates points to some kind of halo effect due to the use of a set of relatively similar rating scales. The study shows that in all the four countries the scale measuring P and M leader styles have high social desirability. At the same time the data shows that the specific meanings of the P and M vary by culture. These studies therefore support the value of Misumi's distinction between general leader attributes and specific ones. They rise the possibility that there may be universal qualities required of all leaders but which Western researchers have failed to find because they have researched for them with measures which are too static and individualistic. Likewise, the findings support the view that by studying the specific actions of leaders and their associates, rather than generalized measures of style, we can better understand the reciprocal interplay, which is their cultural context.

Dr. Bashir Khadra (1982) has developed a leadership model called, "The Prophetic-Caliphal model of Leadership". He has tested empirically the various dimensions of Arab leadership in social and organisational context by conducting a sample survey among 75 managers from the top, middle and lower levels in the administration of the Greater Amman Municipality, Jordan. The model consists of four elements, viz. personalism, individualism, lack of institutionalization and the importance of great man and the two sub-models are the 'prophetic model' and 'caliphal model'. The four elements and two sub-models are highly interdependent and tied together in a comprehensive, dynamic system of leadership relationships. He distinguishes the great man (leader under prophetic model) and the ordinary man (leader under caliphal model) on the basis of the followers' attitude towards the leaders. If they view the leader as distinctly superior to all others, they consider him as a 'great man' or 'prophetic leader'. On the other hand, others as 'average' or similar in his qualities to most others regard the ordinary man; and he is considered as 'caliphal leader'. He concludes that, leadership is given prominence over other factors in development and efforts should be made to realise the significance of institutionalization, which is useful to avoid the dysfunctional influences of the prophetic-caliphal model. He suggests, extensive programme in socio-political and *theological training in democracy* to be conducted so that, it may reduce the degree of personalism, individualism, and the dependence on the great man, as a result the institutions may become well rooted in the society.

RESEARCH IN INDIA

A salient point with regard to Indian research is that most of the studies are on leadership at the lower and middle management level. They have generally tried to classify leaders into the Ohio classification, or the Michigan styles, or have been based on Likerts, Argyris's models (Pathak, 1980, Sinha Jai,

1983-84), Pratap and Srivastave (1980) studied the impact that situational demands have on leadership styles and effectiveness. Singh (1987) and Singh (1983) have used the LPC construct. Ansari and Shukla (1985) assessed the changes in leadership perceptions due to the performance of the group and the behaviour of the leader.

Jauharilal (1983) related leadership styles and decision-making, while Maheshwari (1980) studied the association between decision styles, specifically, participative and entrepreneurial, and organizational effectiveness; Muttayya and Vijayakumar (1985) identified the leadership styles among scientific personnel, and associations with job factors and need satisfaction. All these studies have been as mentioned earlier at the middle and lower levels. There have also been some India-specific typologies generated, for instance the Nurturant Task Leaders, Ansari (1986), Sinha (1987) and Singh (1987), to name a few.

Singh (1990) studied the Indian Management culture, based upon a sample of 176 managers from 56 organisations. The analysis of results shows that typical senior-level Indian manager has an inclination towards the consultative or participative style of management. However, the typical general manager is characterised by relatively more power-oriented than departmental head. A typical Indian manager emphasizes loyalty and belongingness, and is caring in his attitudes. Among the functional managers, the typical marketing manager tends to be highly assertive and individualistic. However, he performs the consultative or participative style of management and does not feel tense at work, despite his high concern for earnings and advancement. Against this the production manager appears to be more caring in his attitudes and is more concerned about cooperative colleagues in the work place with high earnings or advancement. It is interesting to note that all Indian managers tend to put relatively low premium on their personal and family time.

Singh and Dass (1977) studied leadership styles of 280 Indian managers based on a sample drawn from six industrial enterprises. The data were collected with the aid of a structural questionnaire of Reddin's 3-D Theory. The analysis reveals that bureaucratic style is most predominant among Indian managers, followed by the benevolent autocratic, developer and democratic styles, in that order. It also indicates the absence of a clear-cut direction in the managerial behaviour, thereby reflecting lack of managerial convictions and values. In the public sector, there is a preponderance of bureaucratic style, followed by a compromiser, developer and an autocrat. In the private sector, the benevolent autocrat is the most pronounced style followed by the bureaucrat, democrat and developer. A further analysis shows that the benevolent autocratic style is dominated at the top management level and the bureaucratic style at the middle and lower-management levels.

A study on transformational leadership was by Singh and Bhandarkar (1990) who have tried to study the transformational style in times of major changes in five organizations, three in the public, one in the private and one in the corporate sector, in a highly Indianised context. They identified three stages through which the leader of the company goes to facilitate transformation.

Dwivedi (1982) studied leadership crisis among Indian executives. A sample of 128 respondents from seven organisations (public, private and civil service) settings were completed 'Leaders Effectiveness and Adaptability Description' (LEAD) analysis. Based on the analysis of LEAD-self-data, the overall finding was, Indian executives had low leader effectiveness and, thus, faced moderate leadership crisis. The author also found that leader effectiveness correlated negatively with role stress and positively with salary, age and education but none of the coefficient could reach statistical level of significance. There was no relationship between leader effectiveness and experience.

Menon has used 'initiation and consideration' as leadership styles to study effective performance of the executives. Sinha and Sinha have laid emphasis on three leadership styles, viz., 'authoritarian', participative and 'nurturant'. To these three dimensions Habibullah and Sinha have added two more styles, viz. 'bureaucratic' and 'task orientation' styles.

Vinod Malhotra used the critical incident method to derive the qualities of Indian business leaders. He hypothesises that leadership is less about hierarchical authority than inspiration and setting examples. Above all, he observes that leadership involves a set of skills that can be learned. According to him, success in leadership depends on four critical pivots: inspiration, values, change and empowerment.

Hingar conducted a study to find out the variables affecting leadership styles in the Rajasthan State Electricity Board. She administered Leader Behaviour Description Questionnaire (LBDQ) developed by Stogdill. Some of the variables affecting leadership styles included: freedom-initiation, control-orientation and resistance to control. These dimensions do not explain the high variance, which reflects that in the Indian situation taking about only two or three factors will not be of much use. Indeed, in India, the prevailing system of management is paternalistic.

From the above review of literature on the subject, it is clear that Western behavioural scientists were obsessed with the idea as to effectiveness of a leader: Who is an effective leader? What predicts his effectiveness as a leader? To find an answer to these questions they started searching for certain traits such as intelligence, social maturity, inner motivation, achievement drive and human relations attitude, the desire to lead, ambition and energy, honesty and integrity, self-confidence, job-relevant knowledge, etc. When they found through the laborious research the traits did not predict effectiveness, they hit upon the idea that behaviour of a leader-autocratic and democratic would determine the leaders effectiveness. When employee-oriented and task-oriented behaviour failed to throw sufficient light on the effectiveness, Western researchers and behavioural scientists postulated situational or contingency theory of leadership. Fiedlers's Contingency Theory postulated three major situational variables such as, leader-member relations, task structure, and position power.

The very fact that the Western behavioural scientists have reached to the conclusion that the effectiveness of the leader depends upon the situation shows that, there is no specific answer to the question of leadership effectiveness. This is nothing but escapism from the inability to answer the question.

As the Creator, the Almighty God is knowledgeable in every respect; there is a need to search for the divine revelation for understanding the leadership style. Islam is one of the revealed religions, which has word of God preserved in its pristine form without interpolation. Therefore, it is prudent to accept Islamic theory of leadership, which will be presented in the subsequent chapters.

References

Ansari, M.A. (1986), Need for Nurturant Task Leaders in India; Some Empirical Evidence, *Journal of Management and Labour Studies*, 11, 26-36.

Argyle, M., G. Gardner and F. Cioffi (1958), Supervisory Methods Related to Productivity, Absenteeism and Labour Turnover, *Human Relations*, 11: 289-304.

Ayman, R. and M.M. Chemers (1983), Relationship of Supervisory Behaviour Ratings to Work Group Effectiveness and Subordinate Satisfaction among Iranian Managers, *Journal of Applied Psychology*, 68: 338-41.

Barnlund, D.C. (1962), Consistency of Emergent Leadership in Groups with Changing Tasks and Members, *Speech Monographs*, 29: 45-52.

Bass, B.M. (1960), Leadership Psychology and Organisational Behaviour, New York, Harper.

———, (1985), Leadership and Performance Beyond Expectations. New York: Free Press.

Bass, B.M., D.A. Waldman, B.J. Avolio and M. Bebb (1987), Transformational Leadership and the Falling Dominoes Effect, *Group and Organization Studies*, 12: 73-87.

Bennis, W.G. (1976), The Unconscious Conspiracy: Why Leaders Can't Lead, New York: AMACOM.

Bennis, W.G. and B. Nanus (1985), Leaders: the Strategies for Taking Charge. New York: Harper and Row.

Beri, J.C. (1976), Mechanisation, Employment Pattern and Productivity, *Indian Journal of Industrial Relations*, 11: 42 and 44.

Bond, M.H. and K.K. Hwang (1986), The Social Psychology of Chinese People, pp. 213-66, Hong Kong: Oxford University Press.

Bryman, A. (1986), Leadership and Organizations, London: Routeledge & Kegan Paul.

Bryman, A., M. Bresnen, J. Ford, A. Beardsworth and T. Keil (1987), Leader Orientation and Organizational Transience: An Investigation Using Fiedler's LPC Scale, *Journal of Occupational Psychology*, 60: 13-20.

Burns, J.M. (1978), Leadership, New York: Harper & Row.

Carlyle, T. (1907), Heroes and Hero Worship, Boston: Adams (first published 1841).

Chaudhari, *et. al.* (1982), Patterns of Diversification in Larger Indian Enterprises, *Vikalpa*, 7: 23-39.

Cooper, R. (1966), Leader's Task Relevance and Subordinate Behaviour in Industrial Work Groups, *Human Relations*, 19: 57-84.

Davis, K. (1972), Human Behaviour at Work, Tata McGraw-Hill Publishing Co. Ltd., New Delhi.

Dansereau, F.G., Graen and W. Haga (1975), A Vertical Dyad Linkage Approach to Leadership within Formal Organizations: A Longitudinal Investigation of the Role-Making Process, *Organizational Behaviour and Human Performance*, 13: 46-78.

Dholakia (1978), Relative Performance of Public and Private Manufacturing enterprises in India, Total Factor Productivity Approach. *Economic and Political Weekly*, 13: M4-M11.

Dorwin Cartwright and Alvin Zender (1953), Group Dynamics, Research and Theory, New York: Harper & Row.

Dwivedi, R.S. (1982), Diagnosing and Managing Leadership Crisis among Indian Executives. *Lok Udyog*, November 192, pp. 23-35.

Dwivedi, R.S. (1984), A Study of Some Behavioural Determinants of Organizational Performance in Public Enterprises, *Lok Udyog*, 18: 5-16.

Dwivedi, R.S. (2001), Human Relation and Organisational Behaviour—A Global perspective: Macmillan India Ltd., p. 492.

Etizioni, Amitai (1961), Complex Organizations, New York: Holt, Rinehart & Winston.

Farris, G.F. and D.A. Butterfield (1972), 'Control Theory in Brazilian organization', *Administrative Science Quarterly*, 17: 574-85.

Fiedler, F. (1967), A Theory of Leadership Effectiveness, McGraw-Hill : New York.

Fleishmen, E.A. and J. Simmons (1970), Relationship Between Leadership Patterns and Effectiveness Ratings in Israeli Foreman, *Personal Psychology*, 23: 169-72.

Galton, F. (1870), Hereditary Genies, New York: Appleton.

Ganesh (1984), Performance of Management Education Institutions: An Indian Sampler, *International Studies of Management and Organisation*, 14: 197-217.

Greertz, C. (1973), The Interpretation of Cultures. New York: Basic Books.

Habibullah, A.H.M. and J.B.P. Sinha (1980), Motivational Climate and Leadership Styles, *Vikalpa*, 5.

Haire, M., E.F. Ghiselli and L.W. Porter (1966), Managerial Thinking: An International Study, New York, Wiley.

Heller, F.A. and B. Wilpert (1981), Competence and Power in Managerial Decision-making, Chichester: Willey.

Heresy, P. and K.H. Blanchard (1982), Management of Organizational Behaviour; Utilizing Human Resources, Englewood Cliffs, NJ: Prentice-Hall.

Hingar, Asha, (1984), Psychometric verification of Leadership Styles, *Indian Management*, September, pp. 11-19.

Heresy, P. and Kenneth H. Blanchard (1988), Management of Organizational Behaviour Utilizing Human Resources, Printice-Hall International, Inc. USA.

Hofstede, G. (1980), Culture's Consequences: International Differences in Work-related Values, Beverly Hills, CA: Sage.

House, R.J. and T.R. Mitchell (1974), Path-Goal Theory of Leadership, *Journal of Contemporary Business*, 3: 81-97.

IDE International Research Group (1981), Industrial Democracy in Europe, Oxford: Oxford University Press.

Jauharilal (1983), Leadership Styles and Decision-making: The Indian Context. *Indian Management*, Oct. 13-24.

Khadra, Bashir (1990), The Prophetic-Caliphal Model of Leadership: an Empirical Study, *Int. Studies of Management and Organisation*, Vol. 20, No. 3, pp. 37-51, M.E. Sharp, Inc.

Katz, D.N. Maccoby, *et. al.* (1951), Productivity, Supervision and Morale Among Railroad Workers, Ann Arbor, Survey Research Centre, University of Michigan.

Katz, D. and R.L. Kahn (1953), Leadership Practices in Relation to Productivity and Morale in D. Cartwright and A. Zander (eds.) Group Dynamics, Peterson and Company.

Kegan, R. (1982), The evolving Self: Problem and Process in Human Development, Cambridge M.A: Harvard University Press.

Kegan, R. and Lahey, L.L. (1984), Adult Leadership and Adult Development. A Constructive view. in B. Kellerman (Ed).

Kenny, D.A. and S.J. Zacarro (1983), An Estimate of Variance Due to Traits in Leadership, *Journal of Applied Psychology*, 68 : 678-85.

Hotter, J.P. (1982), The General Managers. New York: Free Press

Kuhnert, K.W. and P. Levis (1987), Transactional and Transformational leadership. A Constructive Developmental Analysis. *Academy of Management Review*. 12: 648-57.

Kuhnert, K W. (1990), Journal of Management, Vol. 16, No. 3, pp. 599-600

Lakey, L., Souraine, E., Kegan R., Goodman, R. and Flex, S. (1988), A guide to the subject object interview: Ibs administration and interpretaion, Cambridge, M.A.: Harvard University, *Journal of Management*, Vol. 16, No. 3: 599-600.

Lall (1982), The Emergence of Third World Multinationals: Indian Joint Ventures Overseas. World Development, 10: 127-46.

Lewin, K.R. Lippitt and R.K. White (1939), Patterns of Aggressive Behaviour in Experimentally Created Social Climates, *Journal of Social Psychology*, 10: 271-99.

Liden, R.C. and G.B. Graen (1980), 'Generalizability of the Vertical Dyad Linkage Model of Leadership; *Academy of Management Journal*, 23: 451-65.

Likert, R. (1961), New Patterns of Management. New York: McGraw-Hill.

Lord, R.G., C.L. de Vader and G.M. Alliger (1986), 'A Meta-Analysis of the Relation Between Personality Traits and Leadership Perceptions: An application of Validity Generalization Procedures', *Journal of Applied Psychology*, 71: 402-10.

Maheshwari (1980), Decision Styles and Organisational Effectiveness, New Delhi: Vikas Publishing House.

Malhotra, V. (1998), 'All Fired Up and Ready to Lead', *The Economic Times*, 18 January, p.13.

Mann, R.D. (1959), 'A Review of the Relationships Between Personality and Performance in Small Groups', *Psychological Bulletin*, 56: 241-70.

Mannheim, B.F., Y. Rim and G. Grinberg (1967), 'Instrumental status of Supervisor as Related to Workers' Perceptions and Expectations', *Human Relations*, 20: 387-97.

Meindl, J.R., S.B. Ehrlich and J.M. Dukerich (1985), The romance of Leadership, *Administrative Science Quarterly*, 30 : 78-102.

Menon, S.K. (1975), Leadership and Effective Performance, Shri Ram Centre for Industrial Relations and Human Resources, New Delhi.

Mintzberg, H. (1983), Power in and Around Organizations, Englewood Cliffs, NJ: Prentice-Hall.

Misumi, J. (1985), The Behavioural Science of Leadership (ed. M.F. Peterson). Ann Arbor, Michigan: University of Michigan Press.

Morgan (1980), Paradigms, Metaphors and Puzzle Solving in Organizational Theory. *Administrative Science Quarterly*, 25: 605-22.

Muttayya and Vijaya Kumar (1985), Leadership Styles, Perceived Need Satisfaction and Subjective Job Characteristics Among Scientific Personnel. *Indian Journal of Industrial Relations*, 21: 173-97.

Patrick R. Penland (1974), Group Dynamics and Individual Development, New York: Dekker.

Peter B. Smith and Mark F. Peterson (1988), Leadership, Organizations and Culture, SAGE Publications, London.

Peterson, M.F., H. Maiya and C. Herreid (1987), 'Field Application of Japanese PM Leadership Theory in Two US Service Organisations', Unpublished manuscript, College of Business, Texas Tech. University, Lubbock TX.

Peterson, M.F., P.B. Smith and M.H. Tayeb (1987), 'Development and use of English Language Versions of Japanese PM Leadership Measures in Electronic Plants', Proceedings of the Annual Meeting of the Southern Management, Association, New Orleans, November 1987.

Rensis Likert (1961), New Patterns of Management, McGraw-Hill : New York.

Robert, R. Blake and Jane S. Mouton (1964), The Managerial Grid, Houston, Tex.: Gulf Publishing Company.

Robert, R. Blake *et. al.* (1964), 'Breakthrough in Organizational Development', *Harvard Business Review*, November-December, p. 136.

Robert Tannanbaum and Warren H. Schmidt (1973), 'How to Choose a Leadership Pattern', *Harvard Business Review*, May-June.

Reddin, W.J. (1967), The 3-D Management Style Theory, *Training and Development Journal*, April.

Sadler, P.J. (1970), 'Leadership style, Confidence in Management and Job Satisfaction', *Journal of Applied Behavioural Science*, 6: 3-20.

Singh, R. (1983), Leadership Style and Reward Allocation: Does Least Preferred Coworkers Scale Measure Task and Relation Orientation?, *Organizational Behaviour and Human Performance*, 32: 178-97.

Singh, J.P. (1990), Managerial Culture and Work-related Values in India, Organizational Studies, pp. 75-101.

Singh, P. and G.S. Das (1977), Managerial Style of Indian Managers: A Profile, *ASCI Journal of Management*, September, pp. 1-11.

Singh and Bhandarkar (1990), Corporate Success and Transformational Leadership. New Delhi, Wiley Eastern Ltd.

Sinha, T.N. and J.B.P. Sinha (1977), Differential Profile of Three Types of Leaders, *A.N.S. Institute of Social Studies* (Monograph), Patna.

Sinha, J.B.P. (1981), The Nurturant Task Manager: A Model of the Effective Executive. Atlantic Highlands, NJ Humanities Press.

Sinha, J.B.P. (1984), A Model of Effective Leadership Styles in India, *International Studies of Management and Organisation*, 14: 86-98.

Stogdill, R.M. (1948), Personal Factor's Associated with Leadership, A Survey of the Literature; *Journal of Psychology*, 25: 35-71.

Stogdill, R.M. and A.E. Coons (eds.) (1957), Leader Behaviour: Its Description and Measurement. Columbus, OH: Bureau of Business Research, Ohio State University.

Stogdill, R.M. (1974), Handbook of Leadership. New York: Free Press.

Terman, L.M. (1904), A Preliminary Study of the Psychology and Pedagogy of Leadership, *Journal of Genetic Psychology*, 11: 413-51.

Uma, R.V. (2000), Leadership and Organisational Effectiveness: A Study-based on Selected Organisations, University of Madras.

Vroom, V.H. and A.G. Jago (1978), On the Validity of the Vroom-Yetton Model, *Journal of Applied Psychology*, 63: 151-62.

Weber, M. (1947), The Theory of Economic and Social Organisation, New York: Free press.

Whyte, W.F. and L.K. Williams (1963), Supervisory Leadership: An International Comparison, unpublished paper cited in A.S. Tannenbaum, *Organizational Psychology*, pp. 280-334.

Yukl, G.A. (1981), Leadership in Organizations. Englewood Cliffs, NJ: Prentice-Hall.

Yukl, G. and D. Van Fleet (1982), Cross-situational, Multi-method Research on Military Leader Effectiveness, Organisational Behaviour and Human Performance, 30: 87-108.

3

Theoretical Framework : Leadership Traits and Organisational Chemistry in Islamic Perspective

Leadership can be defined as "the ability to persuade others to seek defined objectives enthusiastically. It is the human factor which binds a group together and motivates it towards goals." (Davis, K., 1980). This definition encompasses the various aspects of leadership while identifying the combination of elements necessary for the emergence of leadership. According to this definition, leadership is perceived, first of all in relation to the leader's personal qualities and skills. Understanding leadership requires that one should examine the attitudes of the group members towards their leaders and explore the source of receptiveness to leadership among group members. Since no leader can emerge without followers, understanding the nature and source of subordination is essential for studying leadership.

The definition suggests that the presence of common goals is fundamental for the emergence of leadership. Leadership emerges in the process of articulating a set of goals and persuading others to commit themselves to achieving them. In addition, goals serve as indicators by which leadership effectiveness can be measured. Though all leaders must be able to articulate a set of goals and mobilize their people to work towards their achievement, not all leaders can succeed in leading their people towards the realization of the established goals. Even though the group's failure to achieve its desired goal is not solely because of the leadership itself, many seem to be interested in and to admire effective leaders due to their excellent traits.

ISLAMIC VIEW OF LEADERSHIP

The trait theory of leadership emphasizes on some basic qualities of a leader such as honesty, sincerity, punctuality and tolerance, etc. By following the below given postulates of Islam, these qualities are developed in a Muslim.

Prayers *(Salah)*

Prayers of Islam help a man to emerge as a leader of a group. Punctuality, piousness and sense of equality are some basic qualities of a leader. Five times offering of prayers in twenty-four hours makes a man well disciplined and punctual. It inspires him to higher morality; serve to purify his heart and soul; suppress evil and indecent inclinations and also generates piousness. In the mosque there is no disparity between leaders and followers. The practice of prayers (five times a day) brings a congenial and friendly relation between the leader and the followers.

Fasting *(Saum)*

The observance of fasting during the month of Ramadan is binding on all adult Muslims. A true leader is one who feels and knows the difficulties and hardships of his followers. Fasting trains a man to realize the problems of deprived people and it also inculcates patience and tolerance, which are most desirable qualities of a leader.

Poor Due *(Zakath)*

It is a social and religious duty of the rich toward the less fortunate or the poorer section of the community, to spent at least 2.5% of one's net savings, as poor due. A successful leader should always be a well wisher of his followers and to look after the weaker section of the group. Payment of *zakah* cultivates a sense of mercy and sympathy towards underprivileged and the weaker section.

Pilgrimage *(Haj)*

Pilgrimage to Makkah is to be performed at least once in one's lifetime, if he is physically and financially able. For a successful leader it is necessary that he should have a broad-based concept of international leadership. For this interaction with cross section of international society is a must. *Haj* provides this opportunity to its performers.

Islam does not postulate on the theory of great man leadership. In Islam, 'Action' (*amal*) is the sufficient quality for a leader. A man who rigorously follows the Islamic principles is bestowed with leadership qualities. There are so many examples in Islamic history. Khwaja Moinuddin Christi was a saint, whose benevolence fascinated the cross-section of society. Islam has its own practical programme through which humanitarian qualities are cultivated in the individual. Murad (1981) says that the law of God regarding the granting of leadership is a law, which has been in operation since the beginning of creation and will continue as long as mankind exists in its present form.

It is said that, power corrupts and absolute power corrupts absolutely. In Islam there is no such danger with the true Muslim leader. Because Islam teaches the leader that he is not a sovereign entity rather he is considered as fully responsible and accountable before his Creator (Allah) for all his deeds and misdeeds. This sense of responsibility and fear of accountability fully protects him from any kind of derailment.

DIVINE AND POPULAR LEGITIMACY

In his paper on the *Seerah*, Mohammed al-Asi has identified three key concepts for leadership, namely, legitimacy, authority and power. The Islamic concept of legitimacy needs further elucidation because it differs fundamentally from other systems. In Islam, there are two types of legitimacies: divine and popular. While most other systems consider popular legitimacy (that is, the will of the majority) as the only determining criterion, Islam requires divine legitimacy (that is, legitimacy acceptable to Allah) as an essential pre-requisite. Divine legitimacy is acquired when the leader obeys Allah and the Prophet, and only then he is entitled to people's obedience. "*O, ye who believe! Obey Allah and obey the Messenger and those charged with authority among you. If ye differ in anything among yourselves, refer it to Allah and His Messenger, if ye do believe in Allah and the Last Day: that is best and most suitable for final determination*" (Quran 4:59). Divine legitimacy thus forms the basis for popular legitimacy. Leadership in Islam must have both divine as well as popular legitimacies; without the first, it cannot have validity; without the second, it remains unfulfilled.

As Allah Himself bestows divine legitimacy, it follows that all Prophets had divine legitimacy. The Quran tells us that only a few Prophets became rulers: Yusuf, (Joseph) Daud, (David) Sulaiman (Solomon) and Mohammed, upon them all be peace. Other Prophets delivered their message but the people, to whom it was addressed, refused to accept it.

Popular legitimacy does not automatically follow from divine legitimacy. It invariably requires a period of struggle but in order for it to be valid; it must be underpinned by divine legitimacy. It also needs emphasizing that the divine message is not implemented in a vacuum: it requires an audience, which is a society, for its actualization. When it is not enforced or enforcible, the mission remains incomplete. In this sense, the mission of the Prophet Mohammed (Sal) was the most successful because he achieved control over a territory where the laws of Islam were fully implemented. The converse is equally true: if the Prophetic message is not fully implemented in society, it remains incomplete. Similarly, popular legitimacy without divine legitimacy is unacceptable and is considered a rebellion against the commands of Allah.

We must now turn to the requirements for leadership in Islam in a more general sense, and the qualities a person must possess to become a leader as well as the tasks he must perform.

PERSONAL QUALITIES AND TRAITS OF A LEADER

The leader's personal qualities and traits contribute the first and most important aspect of leadership. To get a deep insight into the leadership qualities, one has to study and analyse the personality traits of renounced leaders. One of the most elaborate and detailed accounts of leadership traits is that of 'Abdur Rahman'. Ibn Hibban described this man's character in the following terms. He wrote, "Abdur Rahman was overtly forbearing, vastly knowledgeable and sharply insightful, possessed swift decisiveness and strong resolve. [He was] far from inaction, an expeditious and hardworking person who neither enjoyed tranquility nor got satisfaction in indolence. [Hence,] he would not leave the [handling of] affairs to others; yet he would not single handedly dispose of them on the basis of his individual opinion. [He was] courageous and brave, with depth and breadth. [He had moments] of fury, and very few [moments] of serenity. [He was] articulate, eloquent, poetic, perfectionist, easy going, generous and outspoken. He used to attend funerals and pray for deceased. He used to lead congregations whenever he was present at Friday and 'Eid' prayers and to deliver '*khutbah*' at the '*minbar*' [He used] to visit the sick, and come out to meet [ordinary] people and walk in public."(Jabnoun, N., 2001).

This portrayal of 'Abd al Rahman' provides us with a list of some essential leadership traits such as; knowledge, forbearance, intelligence, resolve, diligence, courage, eloquence, generosity, leniency. These personality traits seemed to be shared by many of those who may be described as distinguished leaders, beginning with the most important model of leadership provided by the Prophets. To identify some of the most essential personal qualities of leaders, we specifically trace the moral qualities that the Quran associates with the role of leadership.

Patience and Forbearance

In Islamic culture, patience plays the pivotal role among all the leadership traits. The Quran emphasizes repeatedly the importance of patience for believers in general and for leaders in particular and identifies it as one of the two essential qualities of leadership, and the other being conviction (Yaqin):

"And We appointed, from among them Leaders, giving guidance under Our command, so long as they persevered with patience (Sabr), and continued to have faith (Yaqin) in our signs". (Quran 32:24). As a general quality, patience is manifested in one's endurance in the face of pain and suffering or constant annoyance caused by such natural disaster [divine acts] as diseases, famines, floods or earthquakes, all of which lead to a loss of life and property. As such, patience is manifested in the believer's calm endurance of the traits of life *"Be sure we shall test you with something of fear and hunger, some loss in goods or lives or the fruits [of your toil], but give glad tidings to those who patiently persevere".* (Quran 2:155). However, when the source of pain and suffering is human instead of divine, the Quranic terms for conveying the meaning of calm endurance are resolve (*azm*) and forbearance (*hilm*). Resolve denotes perseverance when confronted with superior human power. A resolute person, therefore, continues to pursue his objectives despite the strong opposition of those who have the power to inflict pain and sufferings. This was the kind of patience with which Prophets persisted in their mission of transforming their communities from the state of corruption to that of truth: *"Therefore patiently persevere, as did the resolute among the Prophets, and be in no haste with them [the unbelievers]"* (Quran 46:35).

The Holy Prophet (Sal) observed; *"Hazrat Moosa (Als) submitted to Allah: May Allah! Which one is the dearest among your creatures? Allah affirmed: that, one who has the power to take revenge yet forgives"* (Miskhat).

Forbearance, on the other hand, refers to one's ability to endure annoyance and irritation even when one has the upper hand over those responsible for producing them: *"For Abraham, was without doubt, forbearing, compassionate and given to look to Allah"* (Quran 11:75).

The Prophet Mohammed (Sal) is reported to have said; *"The strong among you is not the one who overpowers others, but the one who can control him in the moment of anger".* (Muslim).

"So pardon (their fault) them and ask for Allah's forgiveness for them" (Quran 3:159). An outstanding example of the Prophet's patience was demonstrated, following his suffering at the hands of people of Taif in the tenth year of his mission in Mecca. The chiefs of Taif set the hooligans of the town upon him. They

attacked Prophet (Sal) by throwing stones on him. Even amidst the physical and mental pain and agony, instead of seeking revenge the Prophet prayed for their guidance and forgiveness.

Yet another example we could visualise in the life history of Caliph Hazrat Ali (Ral). He who overwhelmed his enemy in a holy war and was about to kill him refrains from doing so. It was not because the poor vanquished begged for his life but because he insulted Hazrat Ali (Ral) by spitting on the Caliph's face. A lesser mortal and a lesser leader would have been roused to great anger and indignation. The arrogant culprit would have been tortured to most painful death. But the true leader who was waging a jihad against untruth and aggression could not indulge in personal vengeance. "If I would kill the enemy under that 'provocation', he argued in his mind, it would have been a murder. To save my act from the slightest tinge of personal grudge, I had no other alternative but to set the enemy free." Here is the unmistakable leadership in its splendid glory. Here is the leadership that ennobled the world, leadership that made the coolest decisions with blood boiling in the veins. (Azam, M.A., 1979)

A manager who is influenced by the behaviour of Prophet Mohamed (Sal) will internalize this value. In dealing with his subordinates, there arise several situations in which a manager gets annoyed and perturbed. However, a Muslim manager handle the situation patiently. For example, when the performance of the subordinate is not up to his expectations, he does not loose his temper; instead he uses persuasive methods to improve the performance of his subordinates.

Honesty and Equality

Leaders are considered honest to the extent that there is 'consistency between word and deed'. They have integrity and do what they say and they say what they do. Quran states, "*O you who are divinely committed! Why do you say that which you do not practice yourself. The worst of you in the sight of Allah is He who says that which he does not practice*".(61:02-03). In the Quran, the Prophet Moses (As) is described as "strong and trust-worthy" by one of the damsels and the Prophet Joseph (As) is described as one who is truthful. Similarly, the Prophet Mohamed (Sal) used to be called *Sadiq* (the truthful) and *Amin* (the trustworthy) during his youth.

During his Caliphate, frustrated well-wishers with a suggestion to bring down the treacherous and usurper Muawiya, his archenemy, by means of some tricks and conspiracy once approached Imam Ali bin Abu Talib. The Imam replied by explaining that the one who fulfils the following three conditions could only exercise divine laws and commands. (Sheriff, A.H., 1984).

- One who does not conspire and play tricks in the affairs of people.
- One who abstains from falsehood and does not wrap the grab of untruth over his action.
- One who does not cast covetous eyes over properties of people.

From the above, we learn that dishonest ways of dealings are anathema at all times even when facing an enemy concealing true nature of one's action and presenting false picture is undesirable and one should never cherish selfish interest in the properties of others. Should he not be free of such base character, he would not command respect and trust of the people whom he leads.

A leader should ensure equality and at no point of time should be left to feel unequal. In an organisation no employee in the same cadre should get any special privileges for whatever reasons. If the manager doesn't keep the balance between what his mind thinks and what his heart suggests, he will be ruining not only his career but also the organisation.

The leader accepts his authority as divine trust of great responsibility. The Quran commands the leader to do his duty for Allah and to show his kindness and equality to those under his authority. *"Those who if We give them power in the land, establish worship and pay Zakath and enjoin kindness and forbid inequity"* (Quran 22:41).

When Imam Ali bin Abu Talib (Ral) appointed Mohamed bin Abu Bakr as Governor of Egypt, he gave him comprehensive instructions in regard to dealings with people during the course of his duties as their leader. The essence is:

- Behave humbly with people.
- Keep yourself lenient and meet with them whole-heartedly.
- Accord them equal treatment so that the affluent do not expect unjustified favour from you. The needy and the poor do not get disappointed of your justice. (Sheriff, A.H., 1984).

Once during his regime as caliph, Imam Ali Bin Abu Talib (Ral) had proclaimed from the prophet that he would not discriminate even by one *dirham* in the process of distribution of *Bayt-al-mal*. All were to be treated equitably from the gathering, Aqueel stood up and yelled and irritably asked whether he (being Ali's brother) was going to be treated on equal basis as a black man in Madina? Being terribly annoyed with such an unfair question, Imam Ali bin Abu Talib (Ral) reacted sharply by asking Aqueel to sit down. He then asked what superiority could be expected in Islam except on basis of *Taqwa* (Piety) provided he had it. In this context the Quran proclaims "*O mankind! We created you from a single (pair) of a male and a female and made you into nations and tribes that ye may know each other (not that ye may despise each other). Verily the most honoured of you in the sight of Allah is (he who is) the most righteous of you. And Allah has full knowledge and is well acquainted (with all things)*" (49:13).

For anyone to suggest discrimination on the basis of colour or status in life was so abhorring to Imam Ali bin Abu Talib (Ral) that it made him react very sharply. He condemned it on the spot even though his own brother among the people present raised it. This shows the paramount importance for a leader to exercise absolute fair play, justice and equity.

Knowledge and Wisdom

Leaders must acquire the necessary specialized knowledge, insight and expertise in the areas in which they exercise leadership, whether it is political, managerial, economical, intellectual, legal, educational or military fields of endeavour. A leader of a commercial firm, for example, should have a general knowledge about his social and political environment, but he also must have mastery over the specifics of his trade. It was

Yusuf's (Joseph's) knowledge that gave him the confidence to step forward and ask Pharaoh to appoint him as treasurer of the realm: *"[Yusuf] said: set me over the storehouses of the land: I will indeed guard them, as one that knows".* (Quran 12:55) Ultimately, however, it is not one's scope of pure knowledge (*Ilm*) that matters in the exercise of leadership, but one's ability to apply the knowledge obtained to practical situations. One's wisdom (*hikmah*) and *ilm* are closely interrupted, though they have slightly different connotations. The term "knowledge" denotes the various ideas one receives about the nature of reality, whereas the term "wisdom" or "judgement" (*hukm*) signifies the way by which knowledge is brought to bear on action. More specifically as is evident in Quranic Chapters (17: *Al Isra*) and (31: *Luqman*), wisdom consists in those principles that guide actions. In *Al Isra;* for instance, wisdom is used in reference in such precepts as "fulfil every engagements" or "pursue not that of which you have no knowledge". It is for this reason wisdom receives special emphasis in the Quran, where it is made abundantly clear that wisdom is a source of blessing and goodness to those who possess it: *"He grants wisdom to whom He pleases, and he to whom wisdom is granted receives indeed a benefit overwhelming. But none will grasp the message but men of understanding".* (Quran 2:269) It is also emphasized that wisdom has been an essential quality of prophets: *"O Yahya! Take hold of the book with might: and we gave him wisdom even as a youth".* (Quran 19:12). *"When he reached full age and was firmly established (in life), We bestowed on him wisdom and knowledge: for thus We reward those who do good"* (Quran 28:14). *"And we strengthened his [Dawud's] kingdom, and gave him wisdom and sound judgement in speech and decision"* (Quran 38:20).

Allah says that the Prophet (Sal) was given both knowledge (*ilm*) and wisdom (*hikmah*), in numerous verses of holy Quran. *"Our Lord! send amongst them a messenger of their own, who shall rehearse Thy signs to them and instruct them in scripture and wisdom, and purify them: for Thou art the Exalted in might the wise"* (2:129). *"It is He Who has sent amongst the Unlettered an apostle from among themselves to rehearse to them His Signs to sanctify them and to instruct them in Scripture and Wisdom although they had been before in manifest error"* (62:2). There are many instances from the prophet's life where his wisdom achieved results that his followers were unable to see immediately. The Treaty of Hudaibiya' illustrates the most striking example in the sixth year of the hijirah; some 1400 Muslims led by the Prophet were prohibited by the Quraish from entering Makkah to perform *Umrah* (offering prayer in the Holy mosque Kahba). The conditions stipulated in the treaty appeared on the face of it to be detrimental to the Muslims and even such close companions as Umar Ibn al-Khatab were unable to understand the true importance at that time, yet it was the Prophet's great wisdom that brought about the treaty whose benefits soon manifested themselves.

In a nutshell, leaders must be intellectual and perceptive, capable of analyzing the overall situation, establishing priorities for action, and developing strategies for their implementation.

In Islamic organizational framework, merit, efficiency and knowledge are given importance. A knowledgeable manager is a source of inspiration to his subordinates. In all occupational matters, the manager guides his subordinates drawing on his knowledge. Knowledge and information are not commodities to be hidden from the subordinates. A manager shares all the information with his subordinates. In any organisation, wisdom of the manager determines the factors like culture, discipline, promotion, and development, etc. of the manager as well as his subordinates.

Eloquence

The ability to articulate ideas and views with clarity and eloquence is another important quality of leadership. Eloquence is important not only for persuading followers to adopt the proposed course of action and committing themselves to a specific set of values and purposes, but also for negotiating and communicating with opponents. The Quran itself is the most eloquent document, which appeals both to the mind and the heart. The Prophet (Sal) articulated the messages of Islam in a way that was immediately accepted by a small group of people in Makkah. Even the Quraish acknowledged that his message had merit, but they opposed it because they viewed it as undermining their personal interest. When Utbah Ibn Rabiah went to the Prophet with offers of money, beautiful women or a position in the Makkan hierarchy, in an attempt to dissuade him from his mission, the noble messenger gave him a patient hearing. When Utbah had finished, the Prophet recited the Quranic verses of the Chapter *HaMim Sajda* (41: 1-54), instead of responding to his suggestions, which clearly imputed ulterior motives to the Prophet. The recitation of the *Surah* had such an effect on Utbah that he returned to his fellow chiefs in utter humiliation, telling them to leave the Prophet alone.

Again, the Quran stresses the importance of eloquence through the example of Musa (Moses) whose reaction, when he received the divine commission to call Pharoah to the way of God, was to plead for the inclusion of his brother Harun (Aaron) in this mission based on the fact that: "*My brother Harun is more eloquent in speech than I, so send him with me as a helper, to confirm (and strengthen) me: For I fear that they may accuse me of falsehood* (Quran 28:34).

In a business organisational situation, a manager with the skill of eloquence can easily attract and inspire the subordinates. With this skill he can articulate the ideas with clarity and command respect in his organisation.

Kindness, Consultation and Leniency

Self-confidence, boldness and courage do not produce effective leader if they are not balanced by kindness, courtesy, and leniency. The latter are the result of the leader's genuine concern for the well-being of subordinates and for those who come under his responsibility and reflect attitude of compassion and humility. It would be quite difficult for a leader who lacks this trait to keep people to his message or interested in him long. It was the Prophet's kindness and good manner that kept the believers attracted to him.

"It is by the mercy of Allah that you have been lenient with them (O Mohammed) for if you had been severe or harsh hearted, they would have broken away from you: so pardon (their fault) them and ask for (Allah's) forgiveness for them, and consult with them upon the conduct of affairs. And when you have taken a decision, then put your trust in Allah. For Allah loves those who put their trust (in him)" (Quran 3:159). The above verse clearly teaches that a good leader shall be kind with his followers that he shall not overburden them, that he shall pardon them if they commit mistakes and ask Allah to forgive them.

Kindness and selflessness prevailed in Caliphs can be seen from the following observation. Hazrat Abu Bakr (Ral) once counselled to Hazrat Umar (Ral). "O son of Khattab! I have chosen you and appointed you as Caliph so that you may deal with them with kindness. You have been a companion of the Holy Prophet (Sal). You know how the Holy Prophet (Sal) used to prefer our interest and that of our family to his family" (Kandhlawi Yusuf, 1985).

Mutual consultation (Shura) is a Quranic command *"and consult them in affairs (of moment). Then, when you have taken a decision, put your trust in Allah. For Allah loves those who put their trust (in him)"* (Quran 3:159).

"And those who answer the call of their Lord and established prayer, and who conduct their affairs by consultation and spend out of what we bestow on them for sustenance" (Quran 42:38). The Prophet himself regularly consulted his companions on all the important matters. It is even more important in the case of leaders. The most outstanding example of Prophet's *shura* occurred on the eve of the battle of Uhud. While he was of the opinion that the city should be defended from within, the majority wanted to go out and fight. The Prophet accepted this; he did not impose his own opinion. There is an important lesson here: the followers' trust and confidence is gained if their opinion is respected. The majority opinion ultimately turned out to be wrong was not used to point accusing fingers. People can be inspired to make sacrifices only if they feel that their opinion is respected and that the leader does not merely dictate to them. In the Battle of Ahzal, the suggestion of the companions to dig a trench as a defense mechanism worked well for the Muslims. (A detailed analysis of Shura is articulated in the next chapter).

The natural corollary to lack of egoistic strivings is that, a Muslim manager who follows the divine guidance does not believe that, his ideas alone are perfect and he alone is right in all situations. He will be lenient and very kind with his subordinates.

Conviction and Politeness

Conviction contributes the base for a leader to perform his leadership task. This is because, the leader's conviction in his mission and purpose lies at the root of all other traits, including resolve and perseverance, knowledge and wisdom, enterprise and eloquence, leniency and forbearance. It is for this reason that the higher the leader's responsibilities and the more volatile the environment in which he operates, the more crucial is his personal conviction in his mission.

When the existing order begins to break down, along with its rules and regulations, actions can be guided only by the principles and values to which one is committed. Thus a deep conviction in and a strong commitment to a set of principles or values are essential for a leader who wants to reform the accepted patterns of behaviour. Again the same conviction is needed if the leader is to challenge the *status quo,* for without a deep faith in a higher and better order, the task of changing the prevalent order is impossible.

Another important trait of a successful leader that stands hand in hand with conviction is "Politeness". A leader should restrain his tongue even if his followers talk or behave in a manner, which is offensive to his temper or taste. He should not utter harsh or offensive speech in retaliation. Instead let the matter pass with tact and gentle conduct. The Holy Prophet (Sal) observed: *"The heaviest thing put in the balance of a believer on the Day of Judgement will be his politeness. Allah looks upon that person with intense wrath who utters indecent and foul speech"* (Muslim).

Hazrat Abdullah Ibn Mubarak (Ral) had defined the virtue of politeness in three ways:

- A person should meet others with a bright, smiling face.
- A man should spend his wealth on the destitute and needy persons.
- A person should not cause harm to any one.

Hazrat Aisha (Ral) reports: The Holy Prophet (Sal) observed: *"The worst man in the eyes of Allah on the Day of Judgment will be the one whom the people avoid on account of his indecent and foul speech"* (Bukhari, Muslim).

Thus conviction and politeness seem to be two ends of a continuum. Naturally a person with strong belief is likely to have strong convictions. These convictions do not make him an arrogant person in dealing with his subordinates; instead he is polite with his subordinates.

Strength and Trust

Leaders must be skilful and trust worthy that is, they must be strong and faithful. The absence of one of these two traits in a leader can seriously undermine organisations. These two pillars are expressed in the following verses, *"Truly the best of men for you to employ is the (man) who is strong and trustworthy"* (Quran 28:26). *"I have full strength for the purpose, and may be trusted"*. (Quran 27:39). *"Yusuf said: set me over the treasury of the Land. I am indeed (trustworthy) skilled custodian and knowledgeable"* (Quran 12:55).

All the above verses are a testimony to the fact that a leader must be skillful and trust worthy: It is certainly not a very easy task to find someone who is highly skilled (full of strength) and highly faithful. On many occasions, we find people who can score very high at one quality but who score very low on the other. Often, one needs to make a choice on which quality supersedes. Following the tradition of the Prophet (Sal), we can easily conclude that the needed skills come first, while faith remain to be required. For example, 'AmrIbn al-'Aas was appointed by the Prophet (Sal) to lead the Muslims, including the great companions of the Prophet, in the Battle of 'Thatu Salasil', just four months after he embraced Islam. This was because 'Amr possesses better military skills than the rest of his army. The Caliphs also used the same criterion. This issue was well explained by Ibn Taymiyya in his book 'Assiyaasah Ash-Shariyah'. A leader with weak or inadequate expertise can bring disaster to an organisation whereas a skilled leader may advance and help the same organisation. Even if the skilled leader is not a strong Muslim, his shortcomings can be made up through *Shura* or the other consultative process of decision-making, Jawdat Sa'eed in his book, 'Work, a skill and a will,' that a weak leader is very detrimental to an organisation while a skilful leader can be very beneficial even if he is faithful enough because his shortcomings can be made up for by controlling him. In fact, the leader does not have absolute power because Islam necessitates participative management and checks and balances.

A Muslim manager is always in communication with his Creator. This ever-lasting and constant relationship with his master relieves him of all the worldly fears. He is free from anxieties associated with a world-wise manager. Since he is trustworthy, he believes his subordinates to be trustworthy. Delegation in such organisation is easy and there exists a healthy and cordial relationship between the members.

Responsibility and Empathy

Leaders shall possess a greater sense of responsibility than the others. A leader shall feel deeply responsible for his followers' well-being. By accepting his position as leader, he has also accepted certain duties. One of the most important duties of a leader is that he is responsible for securing the legitimate rights of his followers. The concept of responsibility is tied to various aspects of leadership in Islam and a leader who fails to take care of one's followers will have to answer for it to Allah Himself. Moreover, 'Accountability' to the creator is one of the basic beliefs of a Muslim. A Muslim manager's terminal value is salvation. Salvation in Islamic system of belief means, that a man is answerable before the Almighty Allah after one's death. There is a life after death. A Muslim's salvation lies in his success in the life hereafter. This value makes a Muslim always feel responsible towards his Creator.

A Muslim believes that, the God creates all human beings including his subordinates and they are the children of Adam and Eve. A manager views his subordinates as not objects to be moved about according to his whims and fancies. He understands his followers' feelings and foresees total empathy in the organization, looks at his subordinates from their angle and views the problems from their viewpoint. In such a climate, decisions are taken in such a way, that everybody feels that it is his decision.

Umar (Ral), the second successor of the Prophet (Sal), once said that he was afraid that a mule might fall in the mountain roads of Iraq and break its legs and God might ask him why the roads had not been paved in that area. (Jabnoun, N. 2001). This demonstrates the extent to which Umar (Ral) felt the responsibility, which in turn made him reach a historically recognized managerial excellence. Umar Ibn Abdul Azees was so careful about the use of everything under his control believing that his responsibility is a source of ignominy and regret in the hereafter. This attitude of Umar Ibn Abdul Azees resulted in an optimum use of the resources of the nation.

Leaders should not only be responsible, rather they should be empathetic towards others. Empathetic managers put themselves in the shoes of others, and are more capable of checking their decisions. Furthermore, empathy promotes trust among subordinates who are likely to reciprocate the empathy of leaders by giving more cooperation. Empathy was one of the main characteristics of Prophet Mohammed (Sal). Allah, the exalted, said, *"Now has come to you a messenger from amongst yourselves; it grieves him that ye should suffer, ardently anxious is he over you: to the believers is he most kind and merciful"* (Quran 9:128).

Justice and Compassion

Justice and compassion are two other essential characteristics a leader must possess. Justice without compassion leads to tyranny, while compassion without justice creates anarchy. Justice demands that all subordinates should be given equal opportunity according to their abilities. A Muslim manager's compassion has no bounds with all his subordinates. A leader needs to maintain a careful balance keeping the overall good of his followers in mind, justly and fairly regardless of their race, colour, origin, or religion. The Quran commands Muslims to be fair even when dealing with those opposed to them.

"O you who believe! stand out firmly for God as witnesses to fair dealing and let not the hatred of others to you make you swerve to wrong and depart from justice, Be just; that is next to piety" (Quran 5:8).

"Allah does command you to render back your trusts to those to whom they are due and when you judge between people that you judge with justice" (Quran 4:58).

"O you who believe! Stand out firmly for justice, as witness. To Allah, even as against yourselves or your parents, or your kin, and whether it be (against) rich or poor" (Quran 4:135).

This is why the Prophet (Sal) emphasized that personal affiliation or other considerations must never compromise justice. In Madinah, the Prophet ordered the hand of a thief to be cut. Some *Sahaba* (companions) thought the punishment would not be carried out because the person was a distant relative of the Prophet (Sal), when he heard this, the Prophet (Sal), assured them that if his daughter Fathima had been guilty, even she would not have been spared. He then reminded them that earlier communities had been destroyed because they had one law for the poor, and another for rich (Hadith-Mishkat). Justice therefore is a fundamental precept of Islam; even more so for a leader because it is part of his responsibility to maintain balance in an organisation. Injustice invariably leads to turmoil and conflict. At the same time, justice must be tempered with compassion. A leader must combine the two in his personality.

Like a true leader of men Caliph Omar (Ral) inflicted on his own son who was found guilty of drunkenness, eighty stripes, according to the prevailing law. The son could not survive the full rigor of the punishment but the dignity of justice, equity and good conscience, which the commander of the faithful had upheld, has made his leadership an unforgettable lesson for the world (Azam, M.A., 1979).

The leadership of Amr Ibn-ul-As offering his own nose to be cut-off in lieu of the nose of a statue which the Christians of Alexandra held sacred but which some miscreants damaged by knocking-off its nose in the darkness of the night. Amr-Ibn-ul-As, the invincible conqueror of Egypt on hearing the complaint from the Bishop tried in vain to locate the culprit. He then offered to repair the nose or even rebuild the statue. But the Bishop would not agree to this proposal nor would he accept money in compensation. He demanded a human nose—a Muslim's nose instead. But Amr-Ibn-ul-As would not lure with money nor force with might even the poorest of his subjects to spare his nose. He was, however, free to offer his own nose and that he did leaving the legacy of a most inspiring leadership that the world has ever known for justice (Azam, M.A., 1979).

Spirit of Sacrifice

Simplicity and self-sacrifice are other qualities that Islam enjoins, especially for a leader because his behaviour has direct bearing on the conduct of others. If the leader is seen to be making personal sacrifices, then the followers will make even greater sacrifices. The leader will soon lose all support if he asks others to do so but himself holds back. Similarly, he must have no personal or class interests. The Prophet, for instance, never did anything to benefit himself or his family. In fact, throughout his life, he made great personal sacrifices. Often he and his family went without food for several days. Once when his beloved daughter Fathima (Ral) asked for a servant to help with household work, he told her that he was sent to secure the *akhira* (hereafter), not to seek the comforts of this world. On another occasion, when Umar (Ral) saw marks on his blessed body, (because the Prophet had been lying on a coarse mat on the floor) he asked why the Prophet denied himself even the small comforts of life when the rulers of Persia and Rome enjoyed great luxury. The Prophet replied that, such comforts are for people who wish to cling to this worldly life. His reply has been a guiding light for sincere Muslims throughout their lives.

Not only did the Prophet personally participate in many battles but in some of the most crucial ones, members of his own family—his uncle Hamza, and cousins Ali and Ja'far—were in the forefront. Hamza was martyred in the battle of Mu'ta. In the battle of Badr, when the Quraish refused to fight members of the Ansar, the Prophet sent Hamza, Ali and Ubaydah Ibn al-Harith to confront them.

There is another area in which the Islamic order is fundamentally different from the predominant secular Western system today. An Islamic leader and those in positions of authority make sacrifices so that the downtrodden would get more. In the West, the elite's live in luxury while exhorting the people to make sacrifices telling them that once the rich get richer, the benefits of prosperity will-tickle down to the poor. In other words, the poor will get some relief. In real life even this is not true; in many rich societies, the poor are becoming poorer. In fact, the poor in the US are poorer than the poor in some of the poorest countries of the world. Islam condemns any system, which allows such disparities; it wants people at the top to make sacrifices so that those at the bottom can have more. Ostentatious living is specifically discouraged; Islam enjoins its adherents to "*Eat and drink* (*of what Allah has provided you*) *but do not be extravagant*" (Quran 7:31). Similarly, it rejects gross inequalities in society, which lead to conflict and ultimately violence. Giving poor due (*Zakah*), at least 2.5 percent every year from the net savings to the needy is another testimony of sacrifice under Islamic culture.

We also find the same kind of simplicity practiced by the Caliphs. Abu Bakr Siddiq (Ral) took a small portion from the *Bait-al-mal* (treasury) for his family's upkeep, because he had to give up his own business when he became the Caliph. On his deathbed, he instructed his family to return to the *Bayt-al-mal* whatever was left of his possession. During Umar's regime, the *Sahabas* wanted to increase his stipend from the *Bayt-al-mal* but he flatly refused despite the Islamic domain having extended far and wide and having acquired great riches. Similarly, Imam Ali (Ral) led very simple life. A bedouin once found him shivering in a worn-out sheet because he would not afford to buy a better cloth to cover himself in. Such examples of self-sacrifice abound in the early history of Islam. These leaders never ordered anything that they did not practice themselves. They were always conscious of the Quranic command. *"O you who are divinely committed! Why do you say that which you do not practice yourself. The worst of you in the sight of Allah is He who says that which he does not practice"*. (Quran 61:02-03).

Prophet (Sal) was a role model. One cannot find difference between his words and deeds. His entire life was substantiating the above Quranic verse. He never preached which he could not practice; to pin point an incident, when a little girl was brought to Prophet (Sal) by her father to advice her not to eat sweets; Prophet (Sal), first stopped eating sweets for few days and then he asked the little girl to do so (Azam, M.A. 1979).

Islamic culture can be described as a culture of sacrifice. "We" replaces the rugged individualism to be found in the Western culture, the self that is totally "I" in the West becomes "We" in Islamic culture. This metamorphosis of self from "I" to "We" demands very heavy sacrifice. According to Islamic theology, Allah has created a human being and given him freedom of choice. At the same time, the Creator calls upon a human being to surrender his freedom. This is paradoxical. A manager influenced by Islamic culture is always on the lookout for sacrificing his individual-self. This sacrifice and surrender before the Creator gives him a feeling of potency. In the act of sacrificing, he experiences potency. He gains by giving, by sacrificing. Western culture encourages taking, receiving, snatching maximum benefits from the business organization. Islamic culture develops and nurtures giving, sacrificing and contributing to the organization in which one works.

Generosity, Chastity and Piety

A good leader needs to have a generous, kind and munificent but discerning heart whereby he does not act with emotions; does not take hasty decisions; nor does he come under easy influence of others who may be trying to poison his ears. Being ever concerned with exercising fairly and differentiating between what is right and what is wrong; he persistently displays forbearance and thinks more while he speaks less.

An ideal and true leader does not have personal interest in his heart or such inclinations and attachments, which are likely to influence his decisions. His primary concern is the welfare of his people or subordinates and pleasure of Allah. He does not worry about what people say or criticize on the mode and course of his action. His motto is always service and not self-interest or self-glory. He acts calmly when faced with any crisis and with farsightedness lest he aggravates a situation. He also aims at maintaining unity among his people even at the sacrifice of his own interest.

A Muslim leader needs to abstain from actions prohibited by Islam and keep away from evil company. Because of the need for him to be an excellent role model for others and to preserve and inspire both in good and bad situations, he cannot allow himself to succumb to worldly temptations. In other words, strength of character is a must. Obviously, a leader whose private life lacks chastity and decency, whose character and conduct is demoralizing and who is devoid of generosity, wisdom and insight would not command the respect of his followers or subordinates.

Imam Mohamed Al Baqr (Ral) narrated that the Prophet (Sal) had said, "Leadership would not impart benefit except of a person possessing three qualities": (Ahmed H. Sheriff, 1984)

- Such piety that prevents him from committing sins.
- And forbearance with which he can control his anger.

- And authority with which he rules (over people in such a way) till he becomes like a kindly father (Sheriff, A.H., 1984).

Obviously a leader with no sufficient piety and fear of Allah which enables one to control his actions is likely to commit such sins and errors that would harm the interests of his people. His impious way of life would debar him from enjoying their respect and confidence. Besides if a leader lacks forbearance and suffers from fits of outrage and anger, he would commit such actions as to harm others and injure their feelings. This would fail him to attract their support and co-operation

An oppressive leader who exercises his authority with show of power causes fear to be aroused and prevents his subordinates from enjoying mental peace and security. A true leader needs to appear like a kindly father and not a harsh authoritarian.

Describing some of the traits of the pious and beloved of God, the Holy Quran says, *"and those who control (their) anger and are forgiving to men and Allah loves the doers of good"* (3:134).

Since a pious Muslim manager is free from all complexes, he does not have reservations in moving with his subordinates. Status, power in an organization is not to be used. Should there be need for exertion (use) of power, he uses it sparingly. This characteristic makes him cheerful and equips him an ability to move from one thought to another. He moves very freely with his subordinates.

ORGANISATIONAL CHEMISTRY

Leadership is a combination of abilities, rather than simply a matter of individual traits. Therefore, focusing on leadership traits alone is not enough for acquiring an intense perception of this phenomenon. Leadership is associated with one's ability to apply personal capacities to the task performed by the group or incorporate the prevailing values and norms among the leader's group with the overall structural and cultural conditions. Even if a person possesses a combination of the abilities discussed above, he may still fail to perform leadership function within his group for various reasons such as, his traits have not been brought to bear on the group's organisational activities or, the inadaptability between the leader's attributes and those of the followers or the message advanced is conceived improperly by the group. Here, we will focus on a leader's personal traits—the first aspect of leadership—and their bearing on the task or role he is expected to accomplish.

Leaders are involved in a variety of activities, such as, planning, directing, coordinating, persuading, controlling, evaluating, etc. while carrying out their duty. Hence, before relating the qualities to the task of leadership, we must identify those activities, which are essential to perform the act of leading. These activities can be broadly categorized as:

1. Directing the members of the group, which includes setting goals for them, identifying the difficulties and obstacles that arise in the way of achieving the set goals, developing strategies for pursuing established goals and finding solutions for overcoming existing problems.
2. Mobilising the resources needed for the attainment of desired goals and development of the competency and skills of the group members.
3. Integrating the different factors required for the continued existence of the group and the unity among its members. (Safi, Louay 1995)

Now, we would examine the task performed by a leader with regard to the above-mentioned activities and the type of leadership qualities needed to establish them.

Direction (Vision)

The first and foremost task that a leader has to perform is providing an appropriate direction to his group. For this, he needs to recognise the specific goals the group has to apprehend and then design a suitable programme to achieve these goals. A leader must see that the goals must be part of a broad vision instead of selecting them in an *ad hoc* fashion, to inspire the commitment of his followers.

A vision statement that contains, a set of goals, an assessment of the group's present and future state and a set of principles to guide the followers' interaction could emerge either by the creative thinking of the leader or by a discussion and exchange of ideas among the members through consultation. Such a statement provides a healthy and harmonious atmosphere for the group members to achieve the desired goals by bringing constancy to the direction and stability to the organisation. It motivates the members to perform with commitment towards the realisation of the goals' reducing or eliminating the confusion, conflicts and misunderstanding among the members and facilitates cooperation between the leader and the followers as well as among themselves. It also serves as a frame of reference for problem-solving activities, which is a crucial aspect of leadership. The problems must be dealt on the basis of an overall vision, whereby they are neither exaggerated nor underestimated and must find a solution that ease the difficulties and facilitate progress towards the ultimate goal. Leaders, regardless of whether the group that they lead is military, business, political, or educational must therefore, be "people of ideas and right concepts".

A leader should have sufficient expertise and knowledge of the group's task to direct the activities of subordinates. Moreover, he must have a perfect understanding of the internal as well as the external environment in which they function.

A leader must exhibit his competency by performing the right task according to their rank and ensuring duties to his subordinates. For example, mid-level leaders are expected to provide technical guidance to their subordinates, while high-ranking leaders should concentrate on strategy, planning and attaining long-term goals. Top leaders should not involve themselves in detailed decisions. On the other hand, they should entrust that task to his subordinates and ensure that details are given adequate attention.

To fulfil the responsibilities of a leader he must implement plans and execute the decisions already made by him. This demands an intense belief in one's mission and a great deal of determination to pursue it despite all difficulties. It was Abu Bakr's strong belief that he was to reinforce and sustain the political order established by the Prophet (Sal) that gave him strength to stand firmly behind his decision to fight the apostates. Though, contemporaries criticized his firmness, it is obvious that such firmness was crucial for the future growth and development.

Finally, the leader's role as a source of diction is connected with their qualities of courage and taking risks, since true leader is not afraid to challenge the existing conditions and bring about changes or improvement in the prevailing atmosphere of the group. That is why; leadership becomes indispensable at the time of crisis rather than at the normal circumstance, where the organisation can function with the help of the established procedures and rules even in the absence of strong leadership.

Mobilization

The second task of a leader is to mobilise the resources needed to achieve the desired goals. Here, the leader has to persuade the group member and generate a strong commitment with them to the proposed vision. In order to persuade the followers, leaders should be good public speakers who can speak with zeal and clarity and convey their message to different groups of people through language that can be understood easily by a variety of audience and should be convincing, moving and aspiring as well. Their message must be challenging that inspires people to exert themselves and invites them to strive for better results.

Effective leaders motivate their subordinates to undertake the proposed mission, by realizing their various interests and concerns and inspiring them with the fact that the ultimate aim of performing a task should be seeking the pleasure of God and by doing so He will fulfil our worldly needs. For realising the interests and concerns of the followers the leader must mingle with them and create a close and personal interaction between the leader and the followers.

Mobilization cannot be achieved merely through communication skills, though ability to put forth a powerful and moving message is very important. Leaders must present themselves an example of exemplary behaviour to their followers. They must uphold their vision through their actions and maintain unwavering commitment to the principles and values they promote. A supervisor who asks his subordinates to sacrifice time or money while exempting himself cannot lay any claim to leadership in Islamic Culture.

An enterprising leader empowers his subordinates by assigning responsibilities and allows them to execute them successfully. By delegating authority to subordinates, a leader gives an opportunity to them to face problems and difficulties and to learn how to overcome them. Naturally, this streamlines their energies and develops their skills and capabilities. Despite the fact that leaders are more experienced, any attempt on their part to monopolize power and decision-making can only lead to a lower level of efficiency. A leader who wants to empower others must be generous, humble, and people-oriented, genuinely concerned about the well-being and development of subordinates. On the other hand, a self-centered, power hungry or envious leader is not capable of that role.

Lastly, mobilizing a group to undertake a new task requires a great deal of determination, patience and perseverance. These qualities of a leader are crucial for overcoming the group's inertia and resistance to change. A leader who fails to get over these constrains through his patience and perseverance will fail to implement his vision.

Integration

After identifying specific goals, providing direction to the group and mobilising and inspiring the group members to pursue and achieve the goals, a leader has to perform the role of a coordinator. He has to ensure solidarity among the followers and maintain the momentum of their progress. To attain this he should create an atmosphere of devotion, satisfaction and trust in the group through effective communication between the leader and the followers. A leader, who gives room for rumour and speculation within his group, ultimately leads the group to an atmosphere of suspicion and mistrust. To prevent this situation a true leader should encourage two-way communication, which ensures an honest and open discussion and exchange of ideas between superiors and subordinates. Important decisions must be taken after having a consultation with the subordinates. Keeping the followers informed about the decisions made and the reasons for making them develops their trust in the leader. To enhance this the followers should be encouraged to participate in the analysis, formulation, implementation and evaluation of important policies. This will improve the commitment of the group members towards the realisation of the objectives and goals. A group, in which such consensual harmony is not sought, would result in stagnation or sudden disintegration due to lack of initiative on the part of subordinates and the crisis developed as a result of the prolonged ex-communicated discontent of the followers.

The leader must show an attitude of caring and sharing to his followers. He demands loyalty and devotion from his subordinates, to the group and the task to be performed. At the same time he must ensure that such a demand is reciprocated by a true concern for the well-being and growth of them. This can be achieved by providing rewards and incentives either in the form of material compensation or due recognition or improvement in status.

Shortly, the true success of a leader lies in making his subordinates feel and act as responsible members of the group, strive for the improvement and growth of the group with the harmonious commitment, and always ready to extent their contribution and sacrifice to pursue their leader's vision.

Leader's Role as a Follower

For executing the leadership task successfully, a leader has to create or reform a group culture, which indeed is a difficult job. Reforming a group means introducing a new vision that has goals and modes of operation distinctly different from the prevailing ones. This presents the leader a great challenge, for he must overcome the inertia and resistance of the members who are accustomed to the prevailing ways. Sometimes, when the desirous leader himself is subject to higher authorities, the defeat of the obstacles within the group becomes impossible.

In the above-mentioned situation, the leader at the middle level of command hierarchy is under moral tension, created by the double role he has to play as a leader and a follower simultaneously. To be a good leader one has to be a good follower. Hence, leaders must be willing to abide by the same rules that apply to their followers. At the battle of the Trench, the Prophet (Sal) worked with those who were digging the ditch. Khalid ibnu Walid, one of the best military leaders in the history of Islam, was always willing to do what ordinary soldiers do. During the expedition of Mutah, he fought as a regular soldier under the command of Zaid ibnu Thabit. At a later occasion, at Umar's (Ral) request, he gracefully agreed to step down as leader of the army but continued to fight as hard in the role of regular soldier as he had when he had commanded the Muslim army (Safi Louay, 1995).

While, one carries out the roles of a leader and a follower at the same time, there is a possibility of clash between the two roles. A visionary and enterprising leader tries to bring forth his vision and the shortcomings and drawbacks of the existing system to the notice of his superior. He opposes strongly certain approaches and modes of activities, and persuade his superiors of the need of changing them, and quite often let himself be considered or interpreted as disloyal in the eyes of his superior and get ignored by them. But a sincere leader has to accept this fate.

As per the Islamic understanding, every human being plays the roles of a leader and a follower. Leadership is a divine sanction bestowed upon each individual. As a follower, one is expected to obey God, and follow the footsteps of his Prophet (Sal) in every deed. Abu Bakr (Ral), the first Caliph said: "Obey me so long as I obey God and his Prophet (Sal). But if I disobey God or the Prophet (Sal), I shall no longer be entitled to your obedience". The success of a leader lies in his ability to maintain a right balance between being a good leader and a true follower, simultaneously.

Thus, it is clear that, as outlined in the Quran and Sunnah, true leadership does not simply lie in the personal traits that a leader possesses. It has a discerning sense in how these traits are incorporated with the task of leadership. Certain qualities such as eloquence, courage, leniency, resolve, etc. gain the status of leadership only when they are applied and examined suitably in various leadership functions. This mechanism of interaction between qualities and task is specified in the Quran and Sunnah. Through *Iman* a Muslim achieves these qualities and the mechanism of interaction with specific context as well as with his subordinates.

References

Ahmed H. Sheriff (1984), The Ideal Leadership : Bilal Muslim Mission, Kenya, pp. 9-11.

Al-Buraey, Muhammad (1985), Management and Administration in Islam, By Kegan Paul Interntional Ltd., UK., p. 348.

Andrae, T., (1936), Mohammed : The Man and his Faith, George Allen and Unwin Ltd.

Azam, M.A., (1979), Leadership: Islamic Foundation Bangladesh, Dacca, pp. 2-5.

Azzam, A.R., (1979), Life of Prophet Mohammed, The Islamic Foundation, Leicester.

Bangash, Zafar (2000), The Concept of Leader and Leadership in Islam: The Institute of Contemporary Islamic thought, London.

Beekun, Rafik and Jamal Badawi (1999), Leadership An Islamic Perspective, Amana Publications, Maryland, USA.

Davis, K., (1980), Human Behaviour at Work: Organizational Behaviour, Tata McGraw-Hill Publishing Co. Ltd., New Delhi.

Farah, C.E., (1967), Islam: Beliefs of Observance, Barran's Educational Series, New York.

Fiedler, F., (1967), A Theory of Leadership Effectiveness, McGraw-Hill, New York.

Gardner, H.W. and Gardner, M.J., (1981), Child and Development, Little Brown, Boston.

Gibb, C.A., (1954), Leadership, in Gardner Lindzey, ed., Handbook of Social Psychology, Cambridge, Mass : Addition-Wesley.

Hangrove, E.C., (1966), Presidential Leadership Personality and Political Style : Collies Macmillan, London.

Hermasi, E., (1972), Leadership and National Development in North Africa, University of California Press, Berkley.

Husein Haykal (1993), The life of Muhammed: English Translation by Ismail Raji al-faruqi, Kualalumpur.

Ibn, Khaldun (1967), The Muqaddimah : An Introduction to History, 3 Vols, 2nd edn, trans. by Franz Rosenthal, Bollingdon Foundation, New York.

Jabnoun, Naceur (2001), Islam and Management, International Islamic Publishing House, Riyadh, Saudi Arabia.

Jawdal Sa'eed (1983), Work a Skill and a Will, Damascus, p. 29.

Kandhlawi, Muhammad Yusuf (1985), The Lives of the Sahabah (An English Translation of "*Hayatus Sahaba*" originally in Arabic, Idara Isha'at-e-Diniyat (P) Ltd., New Delhi. Vol. 2.

Kalim Siddiqui (1998), Political Dimensions of the Seerah : The Institute of Contemporary Islamic thought, London.

Lewis, H., (1960), The Arabs in History, 2nd edn., Harper and Brothers, New York.

Mohamed al-Asi (2000), The Prophet and Power : The Institute of Contemporrary Islamic thought, London.

Mohamed al-Asi and Zafar Bangash (2000), The Seerah : A power Perspective : The Institute of Contemporary Islamic Thought, London.

Muhammad Yusuf Islahi (2000), Etiquette of Life in Islam : Markazi Maktaba Islami Publishers, New Delhi, pp. 220, 323.

Murad, Khurram (1981), Islamic Movement in the West, Leicester, UK: The Islamic Foundation.

Quradawi, Y.A., (1960), The lawful and Prohibited in Islam, Hindustan Publication.

Safi, Louay (1995), Leadership and Subordination : An Islamic Perspective, *The American Journal of Islamic Social Sciences,* Volume 12.

Smith, W.C., (1957), Islam in Modern History, The New American Library, New York.

Valdas Anelauskar (1999), Discovering America as it is : Clarity Press Atlanta, USA, pp. 61-66.

Watt, M.W., (1972), Muhammed : Prophet and Statesman, Oxford University Press, London.

Quranic References

(4:59), (32:24), (2:155), (46:35), (11:75), (3:159), (61:2-3), (22:41), (49:13), (12:55), (2:269), (19:12), (28:14), (38:20), (2:129), (62:2), (41:1-54), (28:34), (42: 38), (28:26), (27:39), (12:55), (9:128), (5:8), (4:58), (4:135), (7:31), (3:134).

4

Shura (Mutual Consultation) System

Shura is the Islamic process of consultation among those with knowledge of the issues involved, and is best accomplished by discussion among those most aware of the situation. It is a matter of fact that the four cardinal Islamic principles, namely, personal freedom, justice, equality and human dignity are conceived within the *Shura* framework of administration. The Arabic word "*Shura*" (Mutual consultation) was derived from the words "*Shawir*" (consult) and "*Mashwara*" (consultation) which means collecting of honey from beehive, as it is correlated in the sense of collection and exchange of ideas among the persons before taking a decision (Musleh-uddin, 1999).

The divine book (Quran) must be the guidance to human beings on all their affairs because their first allegiance is to the Creator (Allah). Human inspiration, intellect and judgement for running the affairs of human beings must be based on the authority of the power and wisdom of God (Allah). Unlike human power, the power of God is good and merciful, unlike human wisdom; the wisdom of God is perfect and indisputable

(Al-Muslimat). Based on this fact, the *Shura* system is analysed as below.

SIGNIFICANCE OF SHURA

Consultation performs a significant role in building a successful way of life for the human being, whether it is his personal life or public life. To do any collective work without prior mutual consultation is not only a way of the ignorant but also a clear defiance of the regulation laid down by Allah. The significance of the process of consultation lies mainly on two factors.

Firstly, it is quite obvious that nobody has the right to decide and act accordingly on his own will, on matters concerned with two or more people without consulting them. If the group consists of a very large number of people, then the leader has to consult their representatives and get their opinion. Only a person who considers himself superior to others and is autocratic in nature can take unfair advantage over others. This attitude is immoral, unjust, selfish and unethical, as it attempts to snatch the rights of others.

Secondly, the responsibility of making decisions on matters relating to the rights and interests of others is so great that, the entire blame falls on the decision-maker, if the decision goes wrong. A true believer hesitates rather not dare to bear such a burden all by himself. One who is conscious of the God, the Day of Judgment and the life hereafter never attempts to impose his decisions on others. He consults his group members and takes a just and impartial decision. By Chance, if some mistake arises in decision based on *Shura*, all shares the burden of the responsibility.

Moreover, the *Shura* system of decision-making has the advantages of: (1) creating the 'we' feeling among the members of the group, (2) reducing the magnitude of conflict, hostility and cutthroat competition among the members, (3) increasing the understanding, tolerance and patience towards each other, (4) enhancing an individual's free expression of personality which leads to gratification of his needs, and (5) providing opportunities to project better ideas.

Above all it is a divine guidance given by the Creator, and adhering to this is treated as *ibadah*. God's blessings are always there on such collective decisions.

QURANIC VERSES REGARDING SHURA

It is appropriate to have a survey of the Quranic verses pertaining to *Shura*. The Glorious Quran is the Book of Allah, the Wise and Worthy of all Praise. It becomes incumbent upon each and every person who seeks the dignity of this world and the bliss of the Hereafter to regulate his life according to it to implement its commandments. It is the actual word of Allah, not created but revealed for the benefit of all mankind. In the Holy Quran, by keeping the importance of *Shura* for the benefit of humanity, a separate chapter has been entitled as *Al-Shura* (Quran—Chapter 42); which contains 53 verses.

The two relevant verses about *Shura* appear in the Quran—Chapter 42 (*Al-Shura*) and Chapter 3 (*Al-Imran*). "*Whatever ye are given (here) is (but) the enjoyment of this life: but that which is with Allah is better and more lasting: (It is) for those who believe and put their trust in their Lord*" (Quran 42:36). Hence, human efforts must be directed to make, not only this life better but also the hereafter secure. In the next verse, Quran says, "*Those who avoid the greater sins and indecencies and, when they are angry even then forgive*" (Quran 42:37). After making humans aware of their responsibility the next verse of Chapter *Al-Shura* says:

> "*Those who answered the call of their Lord, and establish regular prayers and whose affairs are a matter of counsel (i.e. they are conducted by mutual consultation) and who spend out of what we bestow on them for sustenance*" (Quran 42:38).

Briefly, all that belongs to a man in this world is just a passing asset of life that passes from one hand to another; but better and more enduring is what is with God. The higher and more permanent gifts that come from Allah's presence are for those who truly worship and serve Allah. They are described by their characteristics (emerged from the above three verses) (42:36, 37 and 38):

(1) They have faith and it follows that,
(2) They trust in Allah, instead of running after false standards or values,
(3) They eschew the more serious offence against Allah's Law, and of course stay clear of any offence against indecencies,
(4) While knowing that they are not themselves perfect, they are ready to forgive others, even though they are sorely tried with anger and provocation,
(5) They are ready at all times to hearken to Allah's signs, or to listen to the admonitions of Prophets of Allah, and to follow the true path, as they understand it,
(6) They keep personal contact with Allah, by habits of prayers and praise,
(7) Their conduct in life is open and determined by mutual consultation between those who are entitled to voice; for example: in private domestic affairs; as between husband and wife, or other responsible members of the household, in affairs of business; as between partners or parties interested, and in state affairs; as between rulers and ruled, or as between different departments of administration, to preserve the unity of administration,
(8) They do not forget charity, or the help due to their weaker brethren, out of the wealth or gifts or talents or opportunities, which Allah has provided for themselves, and
(9) When other people use them despiteful, they are not cowed down or terrorized into submission and acceptance of evil, but stand up for their rights within the justifiable limit.

These verses, in this way enumerate the characteristic features of those whose rewards are with God and refer particularly to those who conduct their affairs by mutual consultation. "Consultation" which is the key-word of the Quranic verse (42:38) suggests the ideal way in which a good man should conduct his affairs, so that, on the one hand, he may not become too egoistic, and, on the other, he may not lightly abandon the responsibilities which devolve on him as a personality whose development counts in the sight of Allah.

Another verse (3:159) in its context reads: "*It is part of the mercy of God that thou dost deal gently with them. Wert those severe or harsh-hearted, they would have broken away from about thee: so pass over (their faults), and ask for (Allah's) forgiveness for them; and consult them in affairs (of moment) then, when thou hast taken a decision, put thy trust in Allah, for Allah loves those who put their trust (in Him).*

Here it may be noted that in the verse (42:38) God is pleased with those who conduct their affairs by mutual consultation and in this verse. He has ordered the Prophet (Sal) to consult the community. From the drift and contents of this verse it appears that it is addressed to the Prophet (Sal) not as a messenger of God but as a ruler of the Islamic State of Madinah, so that it may serve as an example for rulers and leaders to come.

The importance of *shura* (consultation) as a part of Islamic system of rules is widely recognized. The Quran commands the Muslims again and again to take their decisions after consultation, whether in a public matter or a private one. The Quran does not prescribe hard and fast methods. The number, the form of election, the duration of representation, etc., are left to the discretion of the leaders of every age, country and organization. What is important is that the leader should be surrounded by representative personalities, enjoying the confidence of those whom they represent and possessing integrity of character.

EXAMPLES FROM THE PROPHET MOHAMED'S (SAL) LIFE

The procedure followed by the Prophet (Sal) can be studied in this regard. For example, at the Battle of Badr, the Prophet (Sal) selected certain place for his army in the battlefield. Asked whether this decision was according to his own will or by something Divine, he replied that it was his own decision. Then he was advised by the experienced among the community, and particularly by Al-Hubab Ibn Mundhir to change his decision and he did change it accordingly. This incident points out that, though not asked for its opinion, the community may give suggestions and opinions.

If we examine the Battle of Uhud, we can see that it was the Prophet (Sal) who asked for their opinion and acted upon it. On, still another occasion the Prophet (Sal) acted upon his own decision and this is the Treaty of Hudaibiya. The terms of the Treaty being most unfair it was resented by the community and particularly by Umar (Ral), yet, in view of its importance, the Prophet (Sal) accepted it. Though it was humiliating yet it ended in success to which there is a reference in the Quran: *'Verily we have granted thee a manifest victory'* (48:1).

This shows that the leader may disregard the majority if it is necessitated by the situation.

EXAMPLES FROM THE LIFE HISTORY OF CALIPHS

Certain incidents in the life of Caliphs also prove that a leader may act contrary to the majority opinion if necessary.

The first Caliph Abu Bakr, who after the death of the Prophet (Sal) sent a voyage into Syria, under Usama, to seek compensation for the murder of the Muslim emissary. Usama being too young was considered by the community unsuitable for such an important expedition, but the Caliph was adamant and enforced his decision, for the Prophet (Sal) before his death, had nominated Usama for this expedition.

Another incident took place after the demise of the Prophet (Sal) when the Arabs reverted to their former position and refused to pay *Zakat*. Many of the Muslims of Madinah, and even 'Umar', were in favour of showing leniency but Abu Bakr did not agree to it and said, 'By God, I shall fight those who differentiate between prayers and *Zakat'*.

Caliph Umar once asked the people their advice in a matter relating to his wife Umm Kulsoom who had received a necklace of pearls, from the Queen of Rome, in return for some perfume, which she had sent to the Queen as a present. The people held the necklace to be permissible for Umm Kulsoom but 'Umar did not consent to it and sent the necklace to Bait-al-Mal (State Treasury) and she was given only the price for the perfume that she had sent to the queen as a gift.

The following examples show how the religious Caliphs depended on mutual consultation of the public. One such example is that of Caliph 'Umar who was of the opinion that after the conquest of Iraq and Syria, the land should not be divided amongst the warriors as booty but should be made the property of the state so that through its produce and income the essential works of public welfare may be carried out. Some companions opposed this view of the Caliph. When they were not able to arrive at a suitable solution through mutual consultation, the Caliph called a public meeting in the prophetic mosque for general consultation and addressed the public in the following words: "I have not just gathered you here and given you the trouble for nothing. The reason for inviting you is that you should also participate in the trust of the Caliphate, which has been entrusted upon me by you. Undoubtedly, I am an ordinary human being like you. I want that those who opposed my point of view and those who have favoured it to declare it openly. I do not require that you should comply with my point of view only because you are in possession of the Book of Allah (from which you may derive guidance to resolve this issue)".

The Caliph ultimately referred the case to the Quranic verses (59:7-10), which provides for those to come, so the opposition was finally convinced of the wise policy of the Caliph and accepted his decision. It may be noted that Caliph 'Umar, in this case, acted upon the words; *'if ye differ in anything among yourselves, refer it to God and his Apostle, if ye do believe in God and the last day: that is the best and the fairest way to reach a settlement?'* These words appear in the Quranic verse (4:59). This is indeed the most suitable way of settling disputes and differences amicably (Musleh-ud-din, 1999).

From all the above citation it may be concluded that, as a rule, the Caliph has to accept the majority opinion, but if necessitated by particular circumstances he may enforce his own decision. But this should not be without an effort to reconcile the opposition by sound and convincing arguments, as did Abu Bakr and Umar both. Failing this the case must be referred as required by the above-cited Quranic verse, which applies equally to the Caliph and the community. This includes all the ways and means of peaceful settlement of disputes.

FACTORS REQUIRED FOR THE FULFILMENT OF SHURA

The principle of *Shura* must be applied while attempting to solve each and every matter, irrespective of its nature and intensity, that involves a group of people, which may be an organisation, a family, a community, a village, a town or even the nation itself. For a successful way of life, it is necessary to follow this. In the affairs of a business organisation, both the superior and the subordinates must consult one another before making any decision. If the affair is concerned with a family, counsel must be taken from every adult member of the family. In matters pertaining to groups like a community, a village, a city or a nation, it is not practical to consult every individual concerned. In such situations, the leader must consult an assembly of trusted representatives of the people before arriving at any decision.

The rule of counsel by its very nature demands five factors for fulfilment as follows:

(1) Those people, whose rights and interest are involved, must have complete freedom of expression and must be kept fully informed about the details of how their affairs are being conducted. They must also have the full right to protest if they see any deficiency, negligence, or even error in the proper discharge of the duties of leadership pertaining to their affairs. If they, still, find no improvement in the performance of such duties they must have the right to change their leaders appropriately. To manage the collective affairs of the people after stiffing their voice, fettering their hands and feet, and keeping them in the dark, are a clear-cut dishonesty and a complete violation of the implementation of consultation.

(2) The persons shouldering the responsibility of managing collective affairs must be appointed with the express approval of the people concerned. Such approval must be freely obtained without any hindrance, coercion, bribery, temptation, deceit, intrigue or trickery. The true and rightful leader of a

nation is not the one who imposes himself upon it by every possible artifice, but one who is chosen by the people by their own free will.

(3) The advisers to the head of a nation must also have the full confidence of the people and must also prove themselves worthy of holding such honorable position. It is quite obvious that people cannot trust those who gain representation through pressure, financial means, falsehood and trickery.

(4) The people who give their counsel or considered opinion must do so according to their knowledge and conscience with complete freedom of expression of their will. If this is not so, and the counselors give their opinion under duress and against their knowledge and beliefs, then such opinion amounts to dishonesty and treachery completely contrary to the teachings of Islam.

(5) The collective advice or decision arrived at by the principle of unanimity or majority must be accepted without reservation, because if one group is free to follow its whims in spite of listening to the consultative assembly then the process of consultation becomes meaningless and null and void. Allah ordains that the affairs are run by mutual consultation, but does not say that they are consulted in their affairs. Thus, this commandment is not put into practice by merely consulting one another but it is very essential that the actual affairs be conducted according to the decisions reached unanimously or by the majority at the end of the process of consultation. (Al-Muslimat, Islamic Website)

SHURA AND AUTOCRATIC STYLE OF LEADERSHIP

Shura system is based on certain terminal values internalized by a Muslim leader, which is quite different from autocratic style of leadership. The following are the values, which form the basis of a Muslim leader.

1. *Iman (Belief)*: Iman implies belief in *Tauheed* (Oneness of

Allah) and the Prophethood of Mohamed (Sal) and *Ahirah* (life hereafter). The bedrock of Islamic faith is *Tauheed. Tauheed* demarcates between Islamic culture and other cultures. The Quranic verse, *'Ihlas'* enjoins a Muslim to declare, " *Say; He is Allah, The One; Allah, the Eternal, Absolute; He begetteth not, nor is He begotten; and there is none like unto Him"*. (112: 1-4)

A leader with *Iman* will always carry the idea that he is responsible for his action and he is cautious about any instruction given to his followers, as he will be questioned on the Day of Judgment for his each and every action. So, as a divine guidance he consults his followers in matters connected to them.

2. *Islam (The Religion of submission to the will of God)*: After *Iman,* Islam is the second layer of moral personality of an Islamic leader and followers. Islam means the achievement of peace with Allah, within oneself and with the creation of Allah, through willing submission to Him. Islam is a worldview and an outlook on life. It is based on the recognition of the unity of the Creator and of our submission to His will. As God is One and Indivisible, so is life and our human personality. Each aspect of life is inseparable from the other. Religion and secularism are not two autonomous categories; they represent two sides of the same coin. Each and every act becomes related to God and His guidance. Every human activity is given a transcendent dimension; it becomes sacred and meaningful and goal-oriented. As Maudoodi points out so well, "*Iman* is the seed and *Islam* is the fruition". Because of his Iman, an individual's life will be conducted according to Islamic principles. A leader who practices Islam will submit his ego to Allah, and will never see him as supreme. *Consultation* is one of the ways through which one can suppress ego.
3. *Taqwa (Piety-fear or consciousness of Allah)*: *Taqwa* is the all-encompassing, inner consciousness of one's duty toward Him and the awareness of one's accountability toward Him. As pointed out by Maudoodi, "The essence of *taqwa* lies in an attitude of heart and mind

rather than in an outward form." When imbued with *taqwa*, a person's frame of mind, his thoughts, emotions and inclinations will reflect Islam. *Taqwa* restrains a Muslim leader or follower from behaving un-Islamically, whether to community members, to customers, to suppliers, or to anybody else. A person with *taqwa* always *consults* his subordinates.

4. *Ihsan (doing good or excelling)*: *Ihsan* is the love of Allah. This love of Allah motivates the individual Muslim to work toward attaining Allah's pleasure. In a Hadith reported by Abu Huraira, the Prophet Mohamed (Sal) describes *ihsan* as follows: "To worship Allah as if you see Him, and if you cannot achieve this state of devotion, then you must consider that He is looking at you." (Bhukari) The constant feeling that Allah is watching is likely to prompt a person with *Ihsan* to behave at his best and respect his followers by *consulting* them whenever needed.

The above moral qualities of a Muslim leader will make him predisposed towards his subordinates in the form of love. He trusts his subordinates. He delegates authority. He believes that subordinates will use their potential to the maximum extent possible. Delegation in Islamic context does not mean abdication of responsibility. A Muslim leader discharges his leadership responsibilities with utmost care, as he is responsible before the Creator. In *Shura* system decisions are taken jointly in consultation with the subordinates. In the event of disagreement, the leader takes the final decision. A leader in *Shura* system will not be punitive, he will not adopt coercive methods nor does he do things for his personal aggrandizement. He is filled with *Iman, Islam, Taqwa* and *Ihsan,* which make him humble. In *Shura* system a Muslim leader cannot give orders according to his whims and fancies. He is bound by the commandments of Islam.

In autocratic style a manager is always punitive in his behaviour, coercive in dealings with his subordinates. He is egoistic. For such leader personal loyalty is more important than anything else. He does the things, which suits his narcissistic strivings. The methods adopted by such leader are

Machiavellian in nature. Western style of authoritarian behaviour is rooted in the evil characteristic structure of human beings. In Western culture, rugged individualism is encouraged. A human being becomes more and more devilish in this culture. Whereas in Islamic culture, *Iman, Islam, Taqwa* and *Ihsan* influence man's character structure, so that, he develops his full potentials and even he becomes closer to angels.

SHURA AND DEMOCRACY

Abraham Lincoln in his Gettysburg Address described democracy as "government of the people by the people for the people".

Democracy both as a concept and system has ancient roots in Western history, thought, and philosophy. It does not signify merely the procedural measures of choosing political leaders. It is a natural extension of the materialistic philosophy entity whose value is measured in terms of the pragmatic or utilitarian sense of his usefulness to the "state" society and the world. The spiritual aspect of the man's existence, which in his real value, is not stressed in this system. In essence, democracy is no more than an amalgamation of individual who by forming a majority, assume the right and the power to propagate their personal interest, while making minimal concessions to minorities.

This is the reason why such majority minority election, party system, etc. are of paramount importance in Western political systems. Since these systems are based on secular foundation, any concept of justice cannot be real value to the individual or to the society. Indeed the system provides legal loopholes for the strong/majority gratifies their personal interests at the expense of the weak/minority.

DEMOCRATIC LEADERSHIP IN PRACTICE

'Democratic' leadership as is practiced today involves covert domination—the domination of the elite, lifting the common man out of the inner poverty into the leader's world of values. It is dangerous in the long-run because it takes domination underground. Autocratic leadership boldly uses power as a basis for domination. Democratic leadership works more subtly, it brings in psychological inequality and divides people into the more humane and less humane. It takes away basic human attributes intrinsic to all human beings and reserves them for the elite.

Democracy and its Place in Shura

It seems these days democracy has come to mean all things to all men. It has come to be seen as a term of approval for anything good. Consequently many have sought to equate the Islamic principle of *Shura,* i.e. consultation with democracy. These concepts are however, quite different. The need for popular consultation and the reception of majority decision by all participants in the democratic process is discussed here.

Although a *Shura* aims choosing the proper leadership establishing checks and controls over them, and arriving at decision accepted, appreciated, and supported by the public, it is not the same thing as democracy, which seemingly seeks to achieve similar purposes. By definition, *Shura* derives a philosophical perception essentially different from that of democracy. The difference lies in the notion of justice as a concrete fact of existence which man arrives at through his own nature and Divine revelation, and which he endeavours to attain irrespective of his personal desires and interests.

The essence of democracy is the representation of the members of a political or social unit in managing its affairs. Essentially, a simple majority, by a head count of those who participate in the process, constitutes that representation and legitimizes all policy formulations and actions thereupon. Modern democracies are built on this model. Despite the nobility of its concept and many virtues, a major weakness of the model is that an individual considers himself minuscule in the big picture and ineffective in influencing the behaviour of those who are entrusted with the responsibility of leading the unit. Thus, the apathy factor keeps a significant segment of the population from participating in the process. Overall, it is a small but organized minority, comprising of interest groups, opinion makers and the like, that makes decisions for a disenchanted majority by default and charts out its future.

A major characteristic of the Islamic system distinguishes it from all other democracies. It is in the area of legislation. A general rule in Islam is that: Allah does not burden any human being with a responsibility heavier than he can bear. *"On no soul Allah place a burden greater than it can bear..."* (Quran, 2: 286). Formulating laws for other fellow humans is a responsibility that no human being, however brilliant and selfless, is capable to fulfil. Among the major categories of leaders, those masses, either faithfully or involuntarily follow is that elite class of people in power that lays down the laws for others to obey. Unfortunately, they all suffer from the same array of human weakness as those they aspire to lead. None of them is above the fray of his personal desires and predilections, or possesses the breadth of vision necessary for taking into account the whole gamut of issues relating to human life. These human limitations inevitably lead to the conclusion that the need of impartial and balanced legislation can be met only by the one (Allah) who is free from these shortcomings and has sufficient knowledge, power and a comprehensive vision of the entire humanity, generations after generations.

As a method, the system of *Shura* provides the procedure whereby people sit together and deliberate upon important matters to arrive at and be bound by conclusion in the light of the philosophical concepts of justice. If the issue under consideration is not about justice, but as a case of preferring one to the other, there is no harm in adopting measures such as voting, abiding by the point of view of the minority, etc. The same measures could be restored to if the discussion reached a deadlock in the absence of an authentic analogy. But even here, no decision should be taken until everybody had the chance to express his or her opinion and cite relevant evidence.

Shura is in fact, a significant administrative concept that has been mentioned in the Quran. While it has been dealt within to some extent by the revelation, Prophetic practice, as well as the practice of the companions afterwards; have established some guiding principles with regard to this issue, and provided a direction in which this concept could possibly develop. It is a duty of the entire group to participate in the affairs that are of common concern to all its members. The Quranic verse, *"(the believers are) whose affairs are decided by mutual consultation (wa amruhum shura baynahum)"* (42: 38) means, "their affairs—that is, the affair does not belong to an individual, a group or an elite, but it is 'their common affair' and belongs to the community as a whole". One can easily point to the way in which the Prophet (Sal) consulted his companions in all issues of common concern, except in those that were settled by revelation, and to the examples that are abound in the books of history, he consulted his companions prior to the battles of Badr, Uhud and Khandaq. After the Treaty of Hudaybiah had been concluded, he consulted his wife Umm Salamah (Ral) concerning sacrificial animals. His companions, following his example and the precepts of the Quran, deliberated with each other on a number of issues of public importance, including the appointment of a successor to the Prophet (Sal), the appointment of a successor to Umar (Ral) and so on.

Therefore, it can be clearly seen, Islam, in its pristine form, not only enjoined deliberation, consultation and free discussion of pertinent issues, but also related them to belief (*eman*) and put them second in importance to the prescribed prayers (*salat*). In other words, one's belief cannot be a complete one, without observing this particular principle of *Shura*. This opinion is also supported by Fathi Osman who stated that, "*Shura*, or the participation in decision-making by all parties concerned, (was) a consequence of faith in God and an obligation second in importance only to performing prayers to Him".

There is definitely a place for majority decision-making in *Shura*, as far as the majority opinion is not against Quran and Hadith. There are many reasons to substantiate the above statement. Firstly, there are many directives and indications in Islamic legal and political thought that lend legitimacy to the use of the majority principle. It should also be mentioned that *Shura* is, in fact, a method of collective decision-making. It allows all the participants in that process to express their opinions and state the supportive evidence for those opinions. The objective of *Shura* is trying to find an objectively correct opinion on a given issue, guided by Islamic principles. The participants in *Shura* have to state their opinion on a given issue, not on the basis of their preference however, but on the basis of supporting evidence. In Islamic terms, this means that the opinion in question has to be supported by evidence from the Quran, Sunnah or other valid sources.

In case, solution to a matter is not found directly in Quran or Hadith, one has to make *ijtihad*. It is the accepted and approved norm by the Prophet Mohamed (Sal). The following incident illustrates this: Mu'adh ibn Jabal states that when the Prophet (Sal) sent him to Yemen, he asked; "What will you do if a matter is referred to you for judgement?" Mu'adh said; "I will judge according to the Book of Allah." The Prophet (Sal) asked; "What if you find no solution in the book of Allah?" Mu'adh said; "Then I will judge by the Sunnah of the Prophet (Sal)". The Prophet (Sal) asked; "And what if you do not find it in the Sunnah of the Prophet?" Mu'adh said; "Then I will make *ijtihad* to formulate my own judgement." The Prophet (Sal) patted Mu'adh's chest and said: "Praise be to Allah Who has guided the messenger of His Prophet that which pleases Him and His Messenger." (Bukhari).

In fact, the process of collective *'ijtihad'* can only benefit from having diverse opinions and their supporting evidence and arguments involved in the *Shura* process. One can further say that *Shura* is a process of trying to arrive at a correct answer in connection with the issue that is being deliberated upon by those who are qualified to participate in *Shura*. There are several ways, which facilitate this process and increase the probability of drawing a correct answer from the pool of available opinions or possibilities. In order to achieve this, one has to apply and use tools of *ijtihad*, both those that were accepted by our predecessors as well as those that are deemed appropriate by the contemporary generation of scholars. And one of these tools is the majority principle.

Lord Hailsham in his book, "The Dilemma of Democracy" says that the only proper use of the expression 'democracy' is in respect of political sovereignty and nothing else.... Sovereignty can reside in an individual, a selected number of citizens or the whole adult population. Only the last named can be properly called a democracy.

Popular sovereignty means that the people as a whole are the final source of government, authority and legitimacy. Democratic government is 'of the people' in the sense that it is derived from and based on the people's will.

In Islam, sovereignty is for Allah expressed in the mastership of the *Shariah* (divine law) over the will of the people.

"So judge between them by that which Allah hath revealed, and follow not their desires, but beware of them least they reduce thee from just some part of that which Allah hath revealed unto thee" (Quran, 5: 49).

"Allah knows best how long they stayed with Him is (the knowledge of) the secret of the heavens and the earth: how clearly He sees, how finely He hears (everything)! They have no protector other than Him; nor does He share His command with any person whatsoever (Quran, 18: 26).

Whilst the nation is the source of power, it has a limited authority. The nation's authority is restricted by the unlimited powers of Allah.

Thus in the question of *Shura,* although the people have the right to be consulted in everything, their opinion will not necessarily be transformed into law. This is quite unlike democracy where in theory the people are sovereign and their will is transferred into law. The divine law, i.e. Allah's law is sovereign and consultation cannot over-rule it. For example, no matter how many people hold the opinion that drinking alcohol is allowable, the law will not be changed.

Shura carries no weight when it is in opposition to revelation, i.e. Quran and the Sunnah. Al-Imam Bukhari has narrated in his book that: "The *Imams* after the Prophet (Sal) used to consult the reliable knowledge in the permissible matters (*Al-Mubah*) in order to take the easiest of them. And if the matters as explained in the Book of Allah and the Sunnah they would not go further than that".

Mubah is defined as communication from the lawgiver concerning the conduct of the individual, which gives him the option to do or not to do something. As al-Ghazali explains it is established in the express permission of the Almighty God that renders the commission or omission of an act permissible either in religious terms or in respect of a possible benefit or harm that may accrue from it in this world. *Mubah* is one of the five varieties of divine rules (*Sharia*), the others being the obligatory (*wajib, fard*), recommended (*mandub*), abominable or disliked (*makruh*) and the forbidden (*haram*).

Shura cannot change the obligatory into a permissible act; for example, *Shura* cannot make the payment of *Zakat* an optional act. Abu Bakr raised an army to fight those people who wished to do so, because it was still and will always be an obligatory act. Likewise the community cannot make the forbidden permissible, such as receiving or paying interest is allowable; or turn the abominable into the recommended or the recommended into the abominable. The will of the nation as expressed through *Shura* can be turned into legislation in the area of *Mubah,* provided that when the community renders the commission or omission of an act it does so in accordance with the rule of Allah.

SHURA AND DECISION-MAKING

The messenger of Allah, Prophet (Sal) consulted his companions on several issues by practicing *Shura* effectively. However, consultation and decision-making are two different matters. This is due to two reasons. Firstly, the type of opinion in which (*Shura*) consultation is exercised, and secondly, the centrality of leadership in Islam.

In the case of opinion pertaining to legislative matters, it is known by necessity that legislation can only be according to the revelations of the Quran and Sunnah, for the supremacy in the Islamic life is to Allah and *Shariah* and not to the people. Allah has indicated in the Quran *"The command rests with none but Allah: He declares the truth, and He is the best of judges"* (6:57).

If the supremacy were to the people, the opinion of the majority would be valid and binding on the head of state; this would lead to the *halal* becoming *haram* and *vice-versa*. Therefore, the *shura* in legislative matters is restricted to outweighing and favouring one opinion according to the strength of the evidence in the case of plurality of opinions and understandings.

Despite the fact that the strength of evidence is what makes an opinion outweigh the others, the head of state is the sole body with the mandatory power to make that opinion binding and law on all persons.

Evidence for this is extracted from what took place during the peace treaty of Hudaybia; that when the Muslims objected to what Allah's Messenger (Sal) signed with Quraysh, he (Sal) followed the revelation and ignored the Muslim's opinion and objection. Therefore, if *Shura* had any value in this instance, Allah's messenger (Sal) would not have opposed all his companions.

Outweighing an opinion over another on the strength of the evidence is down to the one seeking an opinion and not down to the people; that is the opinion of Al-Imam Shafi expressed in his book Al Risala, "If the ruler were a *mujtahid* (jurisprudent), he should rule only by the opinion which he believes outweigh others".

For instance, in the matter of 'payment of *Zakat*', Abu Bakr looked upon the issue as being the rebellion of a group of subjects, against the *Shariah* laws, whereas Umar translated it as a fight against a strong Muslim faction defying the state, where the state may not be capable of fighting it. Therefore, Abu Bakr legislated by what he deemed to be the stronger opinion than Umar's, and made it binding on Muslims to fight those who refuse to pay the *Zakat*.

The head of state is therefore the exclusive body that has the mandatory power in decision-making and in exacting laws that are binding, for *Shariah* allows for the head of state to have the final say after consultation and execute his opinion, and not that of the *Shura* people.

Islam made the head of state the sole decision-maker, where an opinion, which he alone thinks, outweighs other opinions. He would then make that opinion law and binding; if he adopts an opinion, it becomes law, and all Muslims should obey him. Two *Shariah* opinions say; "The order of the Imam settles differences" and "The order of the Imam is law, openly and secretly". This is what is called the 'Doctrine of Necessity'.

ORGANISATION OF SHURA

Although the practice of *Shura* is well established by the Book of Allah and the traditions of the Prophet (Sal). Islam has not laid down a definitive mechanism for *Shura* with knowledge of the limits, functions and responsibilities of *Shura*, we submit that *Shura* should be formalised, in a consultative forum, i.e. 'Majlis as-*Shura*', wherein the people, as represented by their elected representatives, can formulate their views for the leader to consider.

Is the view of the Majlis as-Shura (consultative council) binding on the Leader?

Almighty Allah has warned in the Quran: "*And consult them in affairs (of moment). Then when you have taken a decision put thy trust in Allah* (3:159).

In the above verse Allah commands His messenger that "when he decides upon a matter, he should go ahead with it and trust in Allah. Thus when the ruler/leader has formed a definite view, which may, or may not, represent the view of the majority, the ruler is to put his trust in Allah.

The opinion of the majority is therefore not binding on the leader in certain areas. When the leader is seeking the strongest opinion on a certain rule, the leader is to be driven by the quest for the strongest *Shariah* opinion and not the view of the majority. In this regard greater weight is given to the strength of evidence rather than the will of the majority. Similarly, when the leader considers the view of the experts and specialists he will take the view, which convinces him, rather the majority view.

However, in the area where the *Majlis as-Shura* has been given the right to formulate its view on administrative (other than *Shariah*) matters, the majority view of the *Majlis* is binding. This is supported by the action of the Prophet (Sal) in the question of going out of Madinah to confront the enemies at Uhad. Eventhough the Prophet's opinion was to stay inside Madinah; Prophet (Sal) accepted the view of the majority.

To conclude, all matters that are legitimate concern of the *Majlis as-Shura,* i.e. administrative (other than *Sharia*) matters, are to be decided on the basis of the majority opinion, irrespective of whether it is considered to be correct or not. In all other matters of *Shura* the correct opinion is sought, whether it be majority or minority. In business organisation, as per the above jurisprudence, matters have to be decided by the majority opinion and the manager cannot take unilateral decisions; nor he can be autocratic in dealing with the subordinates.

Censuring the Ruler/Leader

It is the right of the people to censure the head of the state and all the officers, leaders. It is an important function of the

Shura to ensure that the ruler conforms to the Book of Allah. *"The deen is an advice ... For the sake of Allah, His book, His Prophet and for the leaders of the masses"*.

The people must remain conscious that it is Allah, the Almighty, who must be obeyed, and not the whims and fancies of man. *"There is no loyalty unto the created which involves disloyalty unto the Creator"* (Bukhari).

This is personified in the behaviour of the rightly guided Khalifah, Abu Bakr (Ral) in his first speech as the Khalifah said, "If I behave well support me, and if I falter straighten me".

Umar ibn al Khattab (Ral), in his capacity as Khalifah, said, "Those of you who see in me crookedness must straighten it". One amongst the audience replied, "By God, if we see in you crookedness, we will straighten it with our swords". Umar said, "Thank God, He has created someone in the community of Mohamed (Sal) who can straighten Umar with his sword". Umar later appointed the same man to the court of act of injustice as a judge.

Umar (Ral) exemplified the behaviour of the God conscious ruler. Once, Umar (Ral) declared that none should increase the dowry (mahr) more than 400 dirhams. He was concerned that the dowry was becoming excessive. On descending the pulpit an old lady said, "O! Umar, have you not heard Allah's injunction?" Umar went back to the pulpit and said, "The woman is right and Umar is wrong. I was asking you not to give more than 400 dirhams as dowry. Whoever so wishes may give as much property as he likes."

If the *Majlis as-Shura* disagrees with the ruler over an action from the viewpoint of *Shariah,* the matter is to be decided by the court for the unjust acts. The court consists of a small band of jurists, who are qualified with the ability to make *ijtihad,* thus able to determine whether the ruler has acted in accordance with the divine law. This accords with the command of Allah in the Quran, *"O you who believe, obey Allah, and obey the messenger and those charged with authority among you. If you differ in anything among yourselves refer it to Allah and His messenger if you do believe in Allah and the last day: That is best, and most suitable for final determination"* (4: 59).

In handling the affairs of an organisation, the leader has to exercise his power and take decision in consultation with the subordinates. He cannot be an autocrat as he is subject to the command of God, to consult the community. Thus, in order to work in cooperation with his followers, a leader should follow as a rule, the advice of *Shura*. Only the Khalifah, not by the executive in business, as laid down by Islamic *Sharia* can apply the doctrine of necessity. They are bound to consult their subordinates and take decision on the basis of consensus opinion. However, there is one basic difference between Western conceptualization of democratic behaviour in business organisation and Islamic business organisation. In secular organisation majority (usually more than half of the members present) decides the matters, whereas a Muslim manager should strive for bringing about consensus among the members. Difference of opinion, if any, should be narrowed down to the lowest level. Consensus or closer to unanimity of opinion will be the hallmark of Islamic business organisation. In case, no consensus reached, majority opinion is resorted to. Prophet Mohamed (Sal) said, *"My nation cannot agree upon an error and if conflict persists, be with the majority"* (Ibnu Maajah). Commenting on the above saying, Izetbegovic said that the 'opinion of the majority is an expression of higher common mind. This is because it yields better outcomes than a single person's opinion. This is a declaration of democratic process. Whether it is the Shareholders Meetings, Board of Directors Meetings or Committee Meetings, efforts should be made to iron out the differences.

However there are several decisions which involve *Shariah* dimensions such as production of products considered *haram* by *Shariah* or where the majority opinion is against natural justice and equity where certain business practices and strategies such as pricing policy, wage policy, which are repugnant to the basic principles of *Sharia*. It is the considered opinion of the researcher that ignoring the majority decision the executive can decide on his own, over-ruling the decision of the consultative body. This should not be construed as autocracy of Western conceptualization. In Western culture, autocracy is a trait of a leader, whereas in Islamic culture, it arises out of necessity to safeguard the spirit and tenets of *Shariah*, and natural justice.

References

Abdul Hakim, Khalifa (1987), The Prophet and His Message, Institute of Islamic Culture, Pakistan.

Al-Buraey, Muhammad (1985), Management and Administration in Islam, By Kegan Paul Interntional Ltd., UK. p. 348.

Altalib, Hisham (1993), Training guide for Islamic Workers, 3rd ed., The International Institute of Islamic Thought, USA.

Beekun, Rafik and Jamal Badawi (1999), Leadership : An Islamic Perspective, Amana Publications, Maryland, USA.

Dwivedi, R.S. (1979), Human Relations and Organisational Behaviour : A Global Perspective, Macmillan India Ltd, New Delhi, p. 372.

Izetbegovic, A.A. (1990), Islam Between East and West, 2 nd edn. American Publications, Indianapolis.

Jabnoun, Naceur (2001), Islam and Management, International Islamic Publishing House, Riyadh, Saudi Arabia.

Ja'far Sheikh Idris (2002), Democracy *v.* Shura, YM Online Discussion Forum.

Maudoodi, Sayyid, Abu A'la (1991), The Islamic Movement: Dynamics of Values, Power and Change, The Islamic Foundation, U.K., cited by Rafik I. Beekun and Jamal Badawi, 'Leadership an Islamic Perspective' pp. 20-25.

Musleh-uddin, M., (1999), Islam and its Political System, International Islamic Publishers, Delhi.

Riaz Khan, M. (2002), Shura and Islamic Vision of Democracy, Message International.

Sinamovic, Ermin (2002), Democracy and the Majority Principle in Islamic Legal Political Thought, *The Message International*, Jamaica, April/May.

Sulaiman, S.J., (1999), The Shura Principle in Islam, Al-Hewar Center, Inc. USA.

Taha Jabir al Alwani (1993), Source Methodology in Islamic Jurisprudence, English Edn. By Yusuf Talal Delorenzo and Anas S. al Shaikh-Ali, International Institute of Islamic Thought, USA. pp. 12-13.

Al-Muslimat, Shura: The Mutual Consultation in Shariah, Islamic Software.

Quranic References

(42:36), (42:37), (42:38), (3:159), (48:1), (4:59), (112:1-4), (2:286), (5:49), (18:26), (6:57), (4:59).

5

Islamic Theory of Leadership : Unique Features

In Islamic framework, man is the perfect creature, sublime creation. Quran says, *"We have indeed created man in the best of moulds"* (95:4) Adam, the first man and also the first Prophet according to Islamic thought; was part of nature when he was in paradise. He was sent out of paradise to give little amount of freedom to the human race. This freedom given to man allows him either to recognise the Creator and worship Him alone or to deny His God-hood or split his God-hood. Islam encourages man to choose the first option, that is to recognise Allah as God, accept His teachings sent through the Prophets, as the code of life and to become closer to the Creator, and always communicate with the supreme power. In this culture the progression of man as the perfect moral being is encouraged by sending remainders through the institution of Prophet-hood. Islam has a built in mechanism of taking a human being closer to God by making obligatory on him to pray five times a day, in addition to supplicate Him several times a day. A Muslim is asked to fast a month during a year. This fasting brings a man closer to God. The human being develops orgastic experience during the period of fasting. Man is made to feel that he is a part of entire humanity including his subordinate. For a Muslim, his subordinates are neither objects of subjugation nor objects of oppression. A Muslim develops respect for the feelings, opinions, ideas and decisions of the subordinates. He does not believe that his decisions alone are perfect. He does not arrogate the power of decision-making to himself. He treats his subordinates as equals. He does not develop authoritarian tendencies. He believes that every human being is an object of respect in the eyes of Allah. He does not believe that his superiors are the objects of extreme veneration; object before whom he should subjugate himself. His love towards his subordinates will give rise to feelings of respect amongst his subordinates. Whenever he feels that strivings of egoistic nature arises in him, he immediately becomes closer to God and gets-rid off egoistic tendencies. For example, when Prophet Mohamed (Sal) was delivering Friday sermon, he immediately started speaking that he was a very poor man; he was the man who used to graze cattle. On completion of the sermon when somebody asked why did he say so? Prophet (Sal) replied that the egoistic feeling started developing in him.

Man is an independent being, having both the divine as well as the animal instincts. The God has bestowed him free will to think, decide and act, and has provided guidance through Scriptures and Prophets, which demarcates between good and evil, right and wrong, true and false, just and unjust, and virtuous and sinful. Before venturing into any activity, man, somehow, consults his own conscience and decides according to his will power. If his will power is dominated by the divine instincts, he selects the moral and ethical path. On the other hand, if he allows the animal instincts to dominate the divine instincts in him, he chooses the immoral and unethical route. In the former situation, he derives satisfaction and happiness and leads a peaceful life, though he may not be able to achieve power, position or wealth. Whereas, in the later situation, through unethical means one may temporarily attain more power, position, wealth and enjoyment than others. However, his conscience always pricks him. Irrespective of being wealthy and powerful in the eyes of others, he leads a peaceless life. A feeling of guilt and fear that his illegal activities may come to light at anytime, and his reputation and status in the society may get vanished will always daunt him. Even if he escapes in this world, he will be caught hold of at the Day of Judgment (hereafter).

According to a *Hadith*, on the Day of Judgment, one will not be able to move even a step without answering the following questions pertaining to the deeds performed in the world: (1) How did you spend your life? (2) How did you spend your youth? (3) How did you earn and spend? and (4) How did you make use of the knowledge you acquired? (Tharqueeb).

The Angels in this world are recording each and every deed of a human being. On the Day of Judgment, the mouth will be sealed. Every organ of an individual will be revealing all the actions from the day of his mental maturity till death. The Quran proclaims, *"That day shall We set a seal on their mouths. But their hands will speak to Us, and their feet bear witness, to all that they did"*. (36: 65). Good and bad deeds will be weighed in the 'scale/balance of justice'. In another verse, Quran says, *"We shall set-up scales of justice for the day of judgment, so that not a soul will be dealt with unjustly in the least. And if there be (no more than) the weight of a mustard seed. We will bring it (to account). And enough are We to take account"* (21: 47). Those who possess more good deeds to their credit will enter the Heaven and others will reach the Hell. *"The weighing on that day is the true (weighing). As for those whose scale is heavy, they are the successful. And as for those whose scale is light: those are they who lose their souls because they disbelieved Our revelations.* (Quran 7: 8-9).

The eternal life in Heaven as well as Hell is permanent. The pleasure and happiness in the Heaven is beyond one's imagination; so as the pain and sufferings, one faces in the Hell. About the Heaven, the Quran affirms, *"Say: Is that best, or the eternal Garden, promised to the righteous? For them, that is a reward as well as a final abode. For them there will be therein all that they wish for: they will dwell (there) for aye: a promise binding upon thy Lord"* (25: 15,16).

Regarding the Hell the Quran proclaims, *" Yea, such! But for the wrongdoers will be an evil place of (final) return! Hell!—They will burn therein,—an evil bed (indeed, to lie only)!—Yea, such!—Then shall taste it,—a boiling fluid, and a fluid dark, murky, intensely cold!"* (38: 55-57). *"As to those who are rebellious and wicked, there abode will be the fire: every time they wish to get away there from, they will be forced there into, and it will be said to them: 'taste ye the chastisement of the fire, the which ye were wont to reject as false"* (32: 20).

Every human being is considered to be a manager or leader. This intuition or position is bestowed by Allah, as a divine trait that passed on to man from Him, since he is the Vicegerent (Caliph) of Allah. Moreover, in Islam, teachings and practices are so excellently designed that a true follower of Islam is capable of becoming leader. Islam advocates that man is superior to all creatures and he is born to rule this material world. Everybody performs the function or role of a manager or a leader, while executing, either individual or group activities. In both, the principles of management such as planning, organising, coordinating and controlling are adhered. In case of an individual activity, he plans what, when, where, and how to do. Here, intention (*niyah*) plays a vital role. When the intention is good and not against the divine guidance or the natural justice, then it is considered as 'worship' and is rewarded by the God. According to Quran, the very purpose of the creation of mankind is to worship God. *"I created the jinn and humankind only that they might worship Me"* (51: 56). The remaining functions, namely, organizing, directing, coordinating and controlling are accomplished on the basis of the intention and plan. The very first Hadith of Al-Bukhari states, *"The reward of deeds depends upon the intentions and every person will get the reward according to what he has intended"*. According to another Hadith, a right plan (*niyah*) gets rewarded before its execution and after the completion of the deed; the reward becomes ten-fold or more. (Bukhari/Miskat)

In the case of a group activity, an individual is assigned a job of managing or leading a group for a specific purpose. Here the responsibility of the leader is multifarious. He has to plan for the entire group, with the right intention based on the divine guidance. He has to consult his subordinates at every stage before taking decisions. As consultation is a divine commandment given by the Almighty, His Grace will be incorporated in the decision. This process makes a manager, respect the sentiments and feelings of the subordinates. The leader has to organize, direct and control the group activities in a fair, free and ethical manner. He has to take care of his subordinates, because such an act is considered as "worship", and he gets multiple rewards than a follower. A leader should always remember the fact that, he is the representative of the Almighty, Who bestows this role upon him, and the Creator is watching him and finally he is accountable to Him. "*Every soul be held pledge for its own deeds*". (Quran 74: 38). Hazrat Abu Yaala Ma'qil bin Yaasar (Ral) relates that he heard the holy Prophet (Sal) say: "*A person who is appointed in authority over people and if he does not look-after them with goodwill and sincerity, he will not get even the aroma of Paradise.*" (Bukahari and Muslim).

On the part of the followers, once the leader is elected, it is the responsibility of the constituents, to obey the orders of the leader as long as the order does not violate the divine guidance. Since the leader is the representative of the Almighty, Quran and Hadith give special emphasis in this regard. "*Obey God and obey the Apostle and those in authority from among you*" (Quran 4:59). Prophet Mohamed (Sal) said, "*I counsel you to fear Allah and to give absolute obedience even if a slave becomes your leader...*" (Abu Dawud, Tirmidhi). Hazrat Abu Huraira (Ral) relates that the holy Prophet (Sal) said: '*One who obeys me, obeys Allah, and one who disobeys me disobeys Allah; and the person who obeys the man in authority obeys me, and he who disobeys the man of authority, disobeys me*'. (Bukhari and Muslim).

Regarding the selection or election of a leader, the divine guidance gives no room for one to demand the position of a leader. It should be opted by the group. Allah's blessings always shower on such leader. If the situation warrants, the members can elect a leader. Election of a leader is regarded as a sacred duty and the members use their votes as a trust from Allah only in favour of a person who in their view is pious and knowledgeable and best qualified to discharge the onerous responsibilities of leadership. "*O mankind! We created you from a single (pair) of a male and a female and made you into nations and tribes that ye may know each other (not that ye may despise each other). Verily the most honoured of you in the sight of Allah is (he who is) the most righteous of you. And Allah has full knowledge and is well acquainted (with all things)*". (Quran 49:13).

Thus, whether it is an individual activity or group activity, everybody performs the leadership functions. The summum bonum of the entire activity must be aimed to "Seek the Pleasure of Allah" and thereby having a peaceful and comfortable life in this world and a very enjoyable life hereafter. This is the "Islamic Theory of Leadership", and the style of leadership based on this theory is a unique one.

This theory is universally applicable and successful, irrespective of place and period. Wherever this theory is followed, whether it is a family, or an institution, or a business organisation, or a nation, the leaders and followers will be doing their duties as per the divine guidance. By doing so, everybody derives pleasure by serving others. There will not be any conflict, confusion, ego problem, power politics, corruption and cheating. Everyone will be competing each other in doing good deeds with the intention of getting more reward from the God, instead of getting more money, wealth or reputation in this world. Everybody is aware that, the Creator is constantly watching him, and every right deed is considered as worship. It is quite natural that, if the manager and the subordinates follow this theory totally in an organisation, all will be benefited in both the worlds. The following illustration will substantiate the fact. In a manufacturing concern, if all the employees follow this theory, they will be sincere, honest and serve the organisation to their optimum level. They will consider the organisation as their own and they will have the feeling of "work is worship". Under this situation, no one is needed to supervise the work of the employees for the purpose of monitoring their sincerity and honesty; as a result, the supervisory expenses will be reduced. There will be more production, more sales and more profit. If the employer follows the same theory; he will treat the employees as his own family members; the profit earned through the sincere and hard work of the employees will be distributed to them (after keeping a reasonable share) by way of more salary and other benefits. Ultimately, the employees and the employer will be getting, not only more money, wealth and reputation in this world but also the permanent enjoyment hereafter; as all the activities are considered as worship. All such individual and group activities will derive the same benefit.

In the Islamic history, Caliph Abu Bakr (Ral) regime was considered to be a remarkable period. He followed the footsteps of Prophet Mohamed (Sal) and this theory of leadership. He led a simple life. For his family expenses he drew a very nominal allowance from the state treasury. One day he noticed his wife prepared a special sweet. He asked his wife about the source of money for the sweet. She replied that, she saved a little amount every time from his allowance and prepared the sweet. He calculated the amount saved by his wife and instructed the treasury to reduce his allowance to that extent. Such a leader was a role model to his follower.

Another example can be illustrated from the life history of Caliph Omer (Ral). Once he was delivering a Friday sermon, wearing a new dress made of cloth distributed to him along with every other citizen, from the state treasury, few days back. In the middle of the sermon, one among the audience stood up and posed a question pointing Omer (Ral), who was on the pulpit. He asked, "Oh! Omer! Answer my question. How come you got enough cloth to cover your entire body, whereas nobody else got enough to cover theirs?" [Umar (Ral) had a huge body structure]. Hearing this, Caliph calmly answered, "My son Abdullah who is present amongst you, is the right person to answer this." Then he directed his son to clarify the doubt. Abdullah stood up and stated that, Caliph too got the same measure of cloth as all the others were given, from the treasury and the other members of Caliph's family gave some part of their share to him, so that, he could stitch a fitting dress for him. This incident clearly indicates at least three remarkable aspects during Caliph Umar's (Ral) regime; (1) rule of equity and justice, (2) freedom of speech given to all citizens, and (3) right to get information by a citizen from the ruler.

Yet another incident from the life of Caliph Omer (Ral): When Caliph Omer (Ral) went for a night patrol, he over heard a conversation between a mother and her daughter. The mother was telling her daughter to add some more water to the milk for sale. When the daughter refused to do so, the mother was asking her, whether Caliph Omer (Ral) was looking while she was adding water to the milk. To this the daughter replied, "the Caliph is not looking but the Almighty Allah is watching". By hearing this, Caliph Omer (Ral) was so delighted. Later on Caliph Omer (Ral) made the same girl his daughter-in-law.

Thus from the above incidents, it is clear that, during the period of Caliph Omer (Ral), both the leader and followers had the fear of Allah and they lived for seeking the pleasure of Allah. That is why, his regime was considered as the golden period in the world history.

Prophet Mohamed (Sal) used to love his companions, take care of their feelings, respect them in such a way that everybody believed that he alone was closer to the Prophet (Sal). This is the highest form of love we can see in any community life. This is a model, which is emulated by all the Muslims. This is one of the basic teachings of Islam.

Islamic culture is not just a culture that calls for getting rid of one's ego but it is a culture of sacrifice. The sacrifice is emphasized in every step of a Muslim's life. Examples of sacrifice by *Sahabas* [or] companions of Prophet (Sal) are abundance in Islamic literature. For example, when *Muhajirs* (migrants) from Mecca came to Madinah, the *Ansars* (helpers or residents of Madinah) shared their properties as well as their belongings. This spirit of sacrifice was observed not only when the giver was wealthy and fortunate but also when they themselves were poor and needy. Even, when one was wanting or in dire need of an object, that object was sacrificed for the sake of somebody else in order to seek the pleasure of Allah. The following is an example of true sacrifice of *Sahabas* at the battlefield.

Abu-Jahm-bin-Huzaifah (Ral) narrates: "During the battle of Yarmuck, I went out in search of my cousin, who was in the forefront of the fight. I also took some water with me for him. I found him in the very thick of the battle in the last throes of life. I advanced to help him with the little water I had. But soon, another sorely wounded soldier beside him gave a sigh, and my cousin averted his face, and beckoned me to take the water to that person first. I went to this other person with the water. He turned out to be Hisham-bin-Abilas. But I had hardly reached him, when there we heard the groan of yet another person lying not very far off. Hisham too motioned me in this direction. Alas, before I could approach him, he had breathed his last. I made all haste back to Hisham and found him dead as well. Thereupon, I hurried as fast as I could to my cousin and, in the meantime he had also joined the other two. *Inna lillahi wa'inna ilaihi raajioon*". Many incidents of such heroic sacrifice are recorded in the books of Hadith. This is the last word in self-sacrifice, that each dying person should forego his own thirst in favour of his other needy brother.

The beautiful nature of this sacrifice is that, it is not to show off ones charitable act or to get fame, name, etc. from the fellow beings. The sacrifice is treated as true sacrifice only when it is meant to satisfy his Creator. The summum bonum of sacrifice is to seek pleasure of Allah. The Holy Quran ordains the Prophet (Sal) who declares, *"Truly my prayers and my service of sacrifice, my life and my death, are (all) for Allah, the cherisher of the worlds"* (Quran: 6:162). This total emphasis on seeking the pleasure of Allah in all his deeds and actions subjugates man's egoistic strivings. This makes him a man with a heart full of love, affection, and care towards his subordinates. This is a sublime culture, which exclusively purges all sadistic, egoistic, masochistic and other regressive tendencies.

In this culture, a manager behaves like a mother towards her children. In such organisation there will be cohesiveness, minimal conflicts and a feeling of brother-hood permeating the organisational boundaries. A typical Muslim manager will have no ill will, contempt, malice, and punitive tendencies towards his subordinates. He gets pleasure in their development. The development of the subordinates will be the development of the manager.

In Islamic culture, ethics play a significant role. Ethical values of a leader has a great impact on the followers. According to Islamic philosophy, ethics is the art of purifying the soul par excellence. The essence and proper nature of man's soul lies in his reason. Those actions are right that are performed according to his reason. The spirituality in man is aroused when he loves God and craves union with Him. This love is the highest virtue, for one who acquires it shows a form of religious patience and forbearance with all the created beings. Thus love for the divine brings serenity of soul, freedom of heart and peace with the whole world.

In this culture, a manager tries to brings changes. It is about creating a progressive mindset and raising aspirations of the subordinates. A Muslim manager create shareable vision and guide their followers towards that vision. Fairness, transparency, integrity and ethics define the value system of a leader. A value system is the currency that a leader uses in achieving his goals. Value system directly translates to cost. Higher the value system, greater is the cost that a leader pays to achieve any objective. Value system is the hall mark of a Muslim leader.

In Islamic culture, a leader elevates to the position of a true leader and he serves the follower, remains with them as an open book in his public and private life. A person's private life quite often influences his public life and *vice-versa* and no man can live intermittingly in either life since the same 'mind' and similar attitudes dominates his actions in both the spheres. A leader with Islamic culture is liberal in giving credit to his colleagues, followers and even to his worthy opponents. He is quick to take blame on himself instead of accusing conveniently the other. His leadership qualities are like the properties of genuine gold, keep the possessor of them always in love, respect and dignity even if he looses power or authority. He, as a conscientious person must be alive to his duty, to his parents, his children, his wife, his neighbour, his subordinates or society. A cruel husband, a negligent father or an unsympathetic neighbour an arrogant boss will make a poor leader. *"And be good to the parents and to the near of kin and the orphan and the needy neighbour of (your) kin and the alien neighbour and the companion in a journey and the wayfarer and those whom your right hand possess; surely Allah does not love him who is proud, boastful"* (Quran 5: 25). He never distracts facts in his own favour or against his opponents. He never takes resort to sensationalism to arouse mass hysteria for cheap popularity and cheaper satisfaction derived from a false sense of superiority.

A decision, which is made by a group with pure hearts, free from all complexes, is naturally most effective. In many organisations, decisions reflect the regressive strivings of the managers and their subordinates, who are brought up under Western thoughts. In Islamic culture purity of motive is emphasized. Decisions are made exclusively to seek the pleasure of God. There is sharing of information and knowledge by the superiors with their subordinates. This strengthens the cohesiveness of the group. It is misleading to call this leadership as democratic or participative or people-oriented. These are the concepts drawn on conceptualization of human nature in Western philosophy.

Specifically, the following are the differences between Islamic and Western conceptualization of leadership styles:

Islamic Approach	Western Approach
1. Duty-oriented people.	1. Rights-oriented people.
2. *Falah* (success in life hereafter) is the highest need.	2. Self-actualization is the highest need in the order of hierarchy.
3. Values are given priority.	3. Skills are given priority.
4. Loyalty is an ethical value in Islamic context.	4. By and large treat organizational loyal is an anti-professional value.
5. Compassion is given preferences.	5. Believe in the competitive spirit-survival of the fittest.
6. Harmony and cooperation.	6. Individualism.
7. Islamic mentality is of believing nature.	7. Western mentality is of critical nature.
8. Islamic mind is synthetical.	8. Western mind is analytical.
9. Renunciation detachment is the important values.	9. Too much of emphasis is given for materialistic attachments.
10. Leadership style is based on shura system.	10. Leadership style is based on autocracy and democracy.
11. Man is bound by divine guidance.	11. Man is bound by self-guidance.
12. Moralistic orientation is emphasized in Islam.	12. Pragmatism is the hall mark of Western culture.

To conclude, Muslim's leadership style is built on the Islamic theory of leadership, based on the divine guidance of Quran and Sunnah. It is a unique style as articulated above. Researchers in the field of leadership are searching for a permanent solution to solve various managerial problems based on Western philosophy, which remain unsolved till date. In this context, it is certain that, this Islamic theory of leadership [Seeking the pleasure of Allah] can provide an ever-lasting solution to various managerial problems worldwide.

References

Ahmad, Fazl (1983), Omar The Second Caliph of Islam, Taj Company, Delhi.
Kandhlawi, Muhammad Yusuf (1985), The Lives of the Sahabah (An English

Translation of *"Hayatus Sahaba"* Originally in Arabic, Idara Isha'at-e-Diniyat (P) Ltd., New Delhi. Vol. 2.

Maudoodi, Sayyid Abul A'la (2000), Towards Understanding Islam, Markazi Maktaba Islami Publishers, New Delhi.

Qutb, Muhammad (1982), Islam the Misunderstood Religion, Markazi Maktaba Islami, Delhi.

Yahya, Abu Zakariya (1987), Riyadh-us-Saleheen, (Arabic-English), Kitab Bhavan, New Delhi.

Zakariah, Muhammed (1979), The Teachings of Islam, Idara Isha'at-e-Diniyat (P) Ltd., New Delhi.

Quranic References

(95:4), (36:65), (21:47), (7:8&9), (25:15&16), (38:55-57), (32:20), (51:56), (74:38), (4:59), (49:13), (6:162).

6

Summary and Conclusion

Leadership function has been in operation since the beginning of the creation and will continue as long as the mankind exists. It is the decisive factor in human affairs. Hence, we say that the leader is a basic necessity of a society. In these modern days, the society is bound to evolve and develop a model system, theory, mechanism, and culture through which capable and meritorious persons with high moral values may emerge as able leaders. From this point of view, we do not find any such system or mechanism existing in other "isms"; which are basically built on Western theories of leadership styles.

In recent period, there has been a growing concern that Western theories of leadership styles have not been effective. This is evident from the fact that, many organisations in which these styles have been given very long trial have proved to be ineffective. The following are some of the reasons for this sad scenario: it seems that Western styles of leadership are mostly autocratic; it creates, through comparison, a damaging psychological inequality between men. A leader or manager with autocratic nature is always punitive in his behaviour, coercive in dealing with his subordinates. He acts without consultation. He wants action and results immediately. The subordinates dislike such attitudes of the leader or manager and they tend to withdraw from such a person.

The democratic style of leadership seems to be advantageous in theory, but in practice it is dangerous in long-run, as it takes domination underground. Autocratic leadership boldly uses power as a basis for domination but democratic leadership works more subtly. It brings in psychological inequality and divides people into more humane and less humane. It takes away basic human attributes, intrinsic to all human beings and reserves them for the elite. The bureaucratic style of leadership is a popular type followed in many organisations, which has many demerits. It is characterised as 'machine theory' due to it's over concern with the formal structure of the organisation to the neglect of human dimension. It is a system, the control of which is completely in the hands of officials who are afflicted with egoism that their power jeopardizes the liberties of ordinary citizen. Red-tapism is the biggest defect of bureaucracy. They bluff and bluster. Drunk with power they treat their subordinates with little respect, which leads to demoralization of the subordinates. These are the basic causes for the failure of Western styles of leadership.

The above scenario induced the researcher to find a universally applicable theory for ever-lasting success in the field of leadership. It is common sense that, only the Creator, the Almighty God has complete knowledge about His creation. With regard to the behaviour of the human beings, the direction and guidance given by the God alone is perfect. So there is a need to search for the divine revelation for understanding the leadership style. Islam is one of the revealed religions, which has word of God preserved in its pristine form without any alteration. Moreover, *Shura* (consultation) is a divine guidance mentioned in the *Quran*, pertaining to leadership and decision-making, which needs a detailed study. With this background, the researcher conducted a formulative study about the 'Leadership style and Shura system in Islamic culture' and articulated the viewpoints in the previous chapters. The summary, findings and conclusion of the study are presented as follows:

To summarize (chronologically the five chapters of the study):

The first chapter, "Introduction", comprises of: moral dimensions, background of the study, statement of the problem, objectives of the study, definition of the terms, sources of the study, methodology followed, and the chapterisation.

When we study Islam we find that a true follower of Islam will have the quality to emerge as a leader in every situation. Islam is a complete way of life, in which every aspect of human behaviour has been explained in the light of Quran and Sunnah. A leader with this moral background will shine as a successful leader. The main object of the study is to evolve a universally applicable leadership theory.

With regard to the sources of study: the Quran and Hadith are the original sources referred for this study. Quranic citations in this study are mostly from 'The Holy Quran English translation of the meanings and Commentary by Abdullah Yusuf Ali' and from the meaning of the Glorious Quran, Text and Explanatory Translation by Mohamed M. Pickthall. With reference to Hadith, the name of the books such as, Al-Bukhari, Al-Tirmidhi, Al-Qudsi and Muslim or the compiler is given after each citation. Documents and manuscripts of life history of the rightly guided Caliphs and the companions of Prophet Mohamed (Sal) and the contemporary literature in the form books, journals, articles, reports, etc., information collected by consultation with scholars and personal experiences of the researcher and expertise of his guide are other sources of this study.

The methodology adopted in this study is mainly exploratory or formulative approach. However, descriptive, analytic and comparative methods are also followed. In this study, empirical approach is not adopted due to the following facts: It is believed that empiricism, as a basis of research cannot be relied in the field of understanding and formulating human behaviour. The conclusion based on empiricism is generally not universal and is more applicable to the societies in which, the experiments had been carried out. The Western empirical social science is based upon the assumption that human behaviour is patterned and that these regularities can be scientifically investigated and expressed as generalizations. But numerous studies in this field have explained the social scientists' inevitable bias emanating from personality subjective factors. It is believed that ontological postulations about human nature revealed by the God through the Prophets are the only perfect knowledge. Therefore, the methodology for this study is relied on revealed knowledge found in the Holy Quran and Sunnah.

A brief overview of the research done on Leadership in India as well as abroad is reviewed and presented in the second chapter, "Review of Literature". The following leadership theories and studies have been reviewed. Trait Theory, Behavioural Approach, Ohio State Leadership Studies, Group Dynamic Studies, Likert's Management System, Michigan Leadership Studies, Managerial Grid, Situational Leadership Approaches, Tannenbaum-Schmidt Continuum of Leadership Behaviour, Fiedler's Contingency Theory, House Mitchell Path-Goal Theory, Vroom Yetten Contingency Model, Hersey-Blanchard Tri-Dimensional Effectiveness Model, The Power Influence Theory of Leadership, Attribution Theory, Constructive Development Theory and Transactional and Transformational Leadership Approach. Literature on leadership in different cultures is also reviewed. After reviewing the Western literature on leadership, the researcher observed the following facts:

The Western behavioural scientists were obsessed with the idea as to what predicts the effectiveness of a leader. To find an answer to this problem they started searching for certain traits and formulated 'trait theories', and concluded that, trait do not predict effectiveness. Then they conducted research on the behavioural aspects and developed 'behavioural theories', which also failed to throw sufficient light on the effectiveness. Then they put the blame on the situation and framed 'situational theories', but that too did not yield expected results. There arise a need for searching a universally applicable theory and this prompted the researcher to conduct the study in this area.

"Leadership Traits and Organisational Chemistry in Islamic Perspective" is the Theoretical Frame work of this study, which is presented in the third chapter. Excellent qualities and traits of a leader play a vital role in the success of any organisation. A man who rigorously follows the Islamic principles is bestowed with effective leadership qualities. Islam teaches the leader, that he is responsible and accountable to his

Creator and that teachings prevent him from doing any kind of misdeeds. Some basic qualities such as honesty, sincerity, punctuality and tolerance are naturally developed in a Muslim who follows the Islamic postulates, namely, offering five times prayers in a day, observing fasting for one month in a year, paying 2.5% poor—due every year and performing pilgrimage to Mecca once in his life time. In Islam, there are two types of legitimacies: divine and popular. While most other systems consider, popular legitimacy (the will of the majority) as the only determining criterion, Islam requires divine legitimacy (legitimacy acceptable to Allah) as an essential pre-requisite. Divine legitimacy is acquired when the leader obeys Allah and the Prophet, and only then he is entitled to people's obedience.

The first element of leadership relates to the leader's personal qualities and traits. The following eleven sets of personal qualities and traits are identified, analysed and articulated in this chapter.

1. Patience and Forbearance, 2. Honesty and Equity, 3. Knowledge and Wisdom, 4. Eloquence, 5. Leniency, Kindness and Consultation, 6. Conviction and Politeness, 7. Strength and Trust, 8. Responsibility and Empathy, 9. Justice and Compassion, 10. Spirit of Sacrifice, and 11. Generosity, Chastity and Piety.

A number of incidents during the life period of Prophet Mohamed (Sal) and rightly guided Caliphs are quoted suitably with every trait. Examples of these traits of an Islamic leader, applicable in the practical business management situation are also illustrated.

Leadership is not simply a matter of individual traits, but rather it is connected directly to one's ability to bring the right balance to the application of personal capacities to the task performed by the group. This role of a leader is explained under the heading, 'Organisational Chemistry'. The various functions performed by a leader while executing the leadership tasks are broadly categorized as, Direction (Vision), Mobilisation and Integration. Direction, here means, identifying the specific goals that the group wants to realise and develop the appropriate strategy to achieve them. Mobilisation deals with the activation of resources needed to achieve the desired goals. Here, the leader has to persuade the group members and generate a strong commitment within them to the proposed vision. Integration is a function, ensuring solidarity and cooperation among the followers and maintaining the momentum of their progress by creating an atmosphere of devotion, satisfaction and trust in the group through effective communication between the leaders and the followers. The leader occupies the follower's role when he is in the middle level of command hierarchy. To be a good leader, one has to be a good follower. In Islamic culture, a true follower of the Prophet (Sal) and the divine guidance will be a role model to others. Hence the success of a leader lies in his ability to maintain a right balance between being a good leader and a true follower simultaneously.

The fourth chapter explains the various aspects of "Shura (Mutual Consultation) System". It is a divine guidance bestowed on the decision-makers (leaders) by the Almighty God. The emphasis on consultation is so high that Allah has spared an entire Chapter, by name, "*Ash Shura*" in the Holy Quran (42: 1-53). Hence, the researcher conducted a detailed study on the shura system and presented its various aspects in this chapter. What makes shura unique in the Islamic culture is, its consensus generating mechanism rather than majority or minority influence. Any decision, which has implication for the concern of others, must be made through consultation. Shura system never allows injustice or anything against the Islamic *Shariah* (Rulings based on Quran and Hadith) even if the majority accepts it.

By taking the above doctrine into account, the following aspects of the Shura are illustrated in this chapter: Quranic verses regarding Shura; significance of Shura; the factors that demand the fulfilment of Shura; democracy and its place in Shura; Shura and autocratic style of leadership; Shura and decision-making; different forms of consultation; organisation of consultative council and its functions, and the leader and the council. Examples from the life histories of Prophet Mohamed (Sal), Caliphs and other companions of the Prophet are incorporated.

Consultation is so vital for the successful way of life, like a main pillar for a beautiful building. It is the divine guidance and it is necessary due to three reasons. Firstly, it is unfair to decide alone a matter, which concerns two or more people.

Secondly, autocratic decisions attempt to grab the rights of others. Finally, if the decision is wrong, the collective responsibility falls on the decision-maker.

Autocracy has no place in Islam and the reasons are: creating inequality, curtailing the freedom, coercive in dealing, punitive in behaviour and so on. Democracy and bureaucracy, which are practiced today, seem to be closer to autocracy in practice. Shura system eliminates the drawbacks mentioned above. The basic differences between democracy and Shura are: in democracy, decisions are taken on the basis of majority opinion, though it may be against the divine guidance and natural justice: whereas, Shura never approves such opinions; in democracy, people are sovereign and their will is transferred into law, whereas, in the divine law, Allah's will is sovereign and consultation cannot over-rule it.

While handling the affairs of an organisation, a leader has to exercise his power and take decisions in consultation with his subordinates and try to involve a consensus among the subordinates. It is the hallmark of the Islamic culture. In case no consensus is reached, majority opinion can be considered for the decisions, provided, the decisions should not be against the *Shariah*. In case of doctrine of necessity, the leader can decide on his own, over ruling the decision of the consultative body, in order to safeguard the spirit and tenets of Shariah and natural justice.

This research has attempted to present an Islamic perspective on leadership different from the Western models as is practiced today. This attempt has resulted in the evolution of a theory called "Islamic Theory of Leadership". Fifth chapter offers the unique features of this theory, which are derived from the basic Islamic sources, namely, Quran and Sunnah. In accordance with the Islamic theory, man is the perfect creature of God and His vicegerent on earth. Islam takes the human beings closer to God, by making obligatory on them, to pray five times a day and to fast a month during a year.

God has given him free will to think, decide and act in accordance with the guidance given through scriptures and prophets. Man possesses both the divine and animal instincts, and one who succeeds in defeating the animal instincts against the divine instincts is a true victor, and leads a peaceful life.

According to Quran, on the Day of Judgment, good and bad deeds of every human being will be weighed in the 'scale of justice' and he will enter heaven or hell accordingly.

God has bestowed upon each human being, the gift of leadership as a divine trait. This is evident in the day-to-day functioning of everybody. A good intention (plan) of doing anything as per the divine guidance is rewarded before its execution and after completion of the deed; the reward becomes manifold (Hadith). In a group, a leader has to plan for the entire group with right intension based on the divine guidance and execute the plan in a fair, free and ethical manner, taking care of the sentiments and feelings of his subordinates. It is the responsibility of the follower to obey the leader and perform the duties with commitment and sincerity for a common cause. God will reward these deeds of the leader and the followers surely, in this world as well as in the hereafter.

Thus, whether it is an individual activity or a group activity, everybody performs the leadership functions. The summum bonum of the entire activities must be aimed at 'seeking the pleasure of Allah' and thereby having a peaceful and comfortable life in this world and a blissful life hereafter. This is the 'Islamic theory of leadership' and the style of leadership based on this theory is a unique one.

Findings

The major findings of the study are summarized as below:

(1) The basis of management style in Islamic culture is articulated. In this culture, the focus is on the belief in Allah and in the Hereafter. Everybody is accountable to the Almighty. This belief makes efforts towards efficiency. This culture is based on unity of mankind and the unity of their destiny. It is therefore, a culture of dialogue, openness and co-operation. It is also a culture of participation, which is achieved through consultation, advice, prohibiting the wrong and enjoining the good. It is a culture of discipline, efficiency and order. It is a culture of unity, caring and sharing. It is a culture of justice for all.

(2) As outlined in Quran and Sunnah, the essence of true leadership lies in the fact, how the personal qualities of a leader get incorporated with the functions of the leadership. Through *Iman* a Muslim achieves these qualities and the mechanism of interaction with specific context as well as with his subordinates. Though there are a number of traits or qualities of leaders described by various authors, the researcher has identified about a set of eleven major traits and explained these traits with reference to Quran and Hadith and incidents from the life history of Caliphs and Companions of Prophet Mohamed (Sal). The behaviour of the leaders with Islamic background, under practical business management situation is analysed. From this analysis, it is found that their superb characteristic features reflect not only on their public life but also in their personal life, which makes them role model to their followers. That is the reason why; Michael H. Hart has chosen the leader of the leaders, Prophet Mohamed (Sal) as 'number one', the most influential person in history.

(3) The basic difference between democratic style of leadership and Shura system is elucidated. The basic difference is; in democracy, the voice of majority is taken as granted though the voice is against the natural justice and fair play: but in Shura, the opinion is valid as long as it is not against the Islamic *Shariah* (Islamic law), irrespective of the number of persons who express their opinion.

(4) The researcher fathomed the psychological underpinning of human behaviour in general and that of the leaders, in particular, which constitutes the character structure of the individual. In brief, one has to find a solution to his freedom and freewill out of the two alternatives available. The first one is a progressive solution in which, he has to relate himself to the nature, other human beings and the society, in order to develop a feeling of love towards everything and everybody according to divine guidance. The second one is a regressive solution in which he subjugates

himself to the nature and other human beings, by way of developing egoistic and autocratic tendencies. Islam advocates the first solution and thus makes everyone happy.

(5) The study reveals the difference between conceptualisation of Leadership under Western culture and Islamic culture. Under Western culture, the ultimate aim is to attain power and wealth in this world, which is temporary in nature; whereas, under Islamic Culture, the ultimate aim of a leader and followers is 'seeking the pleasure of God' *(Razae Ilahe).* So this holy concept is the "Islamic Theory of Leadership", and the style of leadership based on this theory is a unique one. Those who follow this theory shall attain a peaceful life in this world and a permanent blissful life hereafter.

To Conclude

The previous pages offer an Islamic perspective on leadership, different from Western theories as practiced today. For more than one century, business concerns across the world tried different forms of organisations such as bureaucratic, matrix, functional, etc. and management styles ranging from autocratic to *laissez-faire;* based on theories, formulations and perceptions of Western theorists. The very evolution of ideas in the field of management on the question of leadership styles bears testimony to the fact that no final view holds good for all times to come and in all situations. Any nation that attempts to follow the exact steps of more developed nations in a pursuit of development ends in failure. Thus in the words of Schumacher (1978) and quoted by Al-Buraey (1985):

> "More and more people are beginning to realise that the modern experiment has failed. Man closed the gates of Heaven against himself and tried, with immense energy and ingenuity, to confine himself to the earth. He is now discovering that the earth is but a transitory state, so that a refusal to reach for heaven means an involuntary descent into Hell".

The Islamic perspective could not be explained in better terms. God, the Creator, did reveal solution to all the problems of man and the main problem lies in man's comprehension and disposition of these solutions. When man himself plays the role of God, then his moral as well as other problems multiply. An important contribution of this research is that it offers solutions to the existing problems related to the leadership concept based on the strong belief in divine guidance. One of the claims of divine guidance found in the religion of Islam is that, it holds good universally as long as the mankind exists. Whether one believes in the universality of these conceptualization or not, the divine guidance deserves a fair trial in business organisations, managed by Muslims or non-Muslims.

Glossary*

Adl	:	Justice, equilibrium, and equity. A fundamental value governing all social behaviours and forming the basis of all social dealings and legal frameworks.
Akhirah	:	Hereafter.
Alaihisalam (Als)	:	May Allah's peace be upon him.
Al Amin	:	The Trustworthy—a name given to Prophet (Sal).
Alhamdu Lillah	:	Praise be to Allah.
Allah	:	Creator and Sustainer of all. Supreme Being. God.
Amale Salih	:	Good deeds.
Amanah	:	Something given to some for safekeeping. Trust.
Amir	:	Leader.
Ansar	:	Helpers—collective title of the people of Madinah who helped the Prophet and his Companions when they migrated from Makkah to Madinah.
Awqaf	:	A trusteeship.
Ayat	:	A section of the text of the Quran referred to

* Glossary of Terms based on Islamic Scholar software, *Taqwa*: The provision of believers (London : Al Firdous, 1996).

		as a "verse". It literally means sign, indication or message.
Azm	:	Resolve.
Bayah	:	A pledge of allegiance.
Bayt al Mal	:	The Muslim public treasury.
Bidah	:	Literally an innovation refers to any act that has no precedent from, or no continuity with, the Sunnah. It has no validity in Islam.
Caliph	:	Khalifah: The leader of the Muslim Ummah.
Dawah	:	Invitation, call. Refers to the duty of Muslims to invite or call other to the straight and natural path of Islam.
Dhiya	:	Waste
Din	:	Religion, a way of life. Used to refer to Islam and the way of life it ordains.
Dinars	:	Money/coins.
Dua	:	Supplication to Allah. Invocation.
Dunya	:	World/Earth.
Falah	:	Success (in life hereafter).
Fardh	:	Some thing which is obligatory. Such as five times prayer daily.
Hadith	:	Narrations and reports of the deeds and sayings of the Holy Prophet (Sal).
Haj	:	Pilgrimage during the month of Dul Haj to Makkah where the Kaba, the House of Allah, is located.
Halal	:	Anything permitted by the Shariah (Islamic Law). Lawful.
Haqq	:	Right. Truth.
Haram	:	Anything prohibited by the Shariah (Islamic Law). Unlawful.
Hidayah	:	Divine guidance.
Hijrah	:	Migration of the Holy Prophet from Makkah to Madinah. The Muslim Calendar begins from the year of the Hijrah of the Prophet (A.D. 622).

Hikmah	: One's ability to put knowledge (*ilm*) into practice.
Hilm	: Forbearance.
Ibadah	: Worship.
Ijtihad	: Islamic method of arriving decision on opinions based on guiding principle when faced with new situation.
Ihsan	: Doing good or excelling.
Ilm	: Knowledge.
Imam	: A person who is leading any of the five prayers that Muslims observe daily. It also means a leader in general, a reputable scholar, or the leader of a Muslim country.
Iman	: Belief in the article of faith enunciated in the Quran and the Sunnah.
Insha Allah	: God willing.
Inna Lillahi Wa Inna:— Ilaihi Raji un	: We remain here for the sake of Allah and will be back to Him (To be recited while hearing sorrowful news)
Islam	: To submit and offer peace. The religion of all the Prophets of Allah confirmed finally by the mission of the Prophet Mohamed (Sal).
Istislah	: Public interest.
Jamah	: Congregation, community or group of Muslims.
Jannah	: Paradise. Heaven.
Jihad	: To struggle. "Any earnest striving in the way of Allah, involving either personal effort, material resources, or arms for righteousness and against evil, wrongdoing and oppression."
Jinn	: Invisible beings constituting a whole race like mankind.
Kabah	: A cube-shaped building built by the Prophets Ibrahim and Ismail (Als).

Khalifah	:	Caliph, Vicegerent, Ruler. "The word Khalifah was used after the death of the Prophet Mohamed (Sal) to refer to his successors, Abu Bakr (Ral), Umar (Ral), Uthman (Ral) and Ali (Ral).
Khilafah	:	Vicegerent.
Khutbah	:	Sermon, especially during the Friday prayer and key Islamic festivals.
ufr	:	Covering, hiding or being ungrateful. In Islam, it means rejecting any or all articles of faith.
Madinah	:	The city in Arabia where the Prophet Mohammed (Sal) is buried.
Majlis	:	Council.
Makkah/Mecca	:	The city in Arabia where the holy Kabah is situated.
Makruh	:	Disliked
Masjid	:	Place of worship.
Mubah	:	Permissible
Muhajirin	:	Migrators, emigrants. Title given to the Muslims who, along with the Prophet, migrated from Makkah to Madinah. Singular *muhajir.*
Mujitahid	:	Jurisprudent
Mumin	:	One who has *iman.*
Munafiqin	:	Hypocrites
Mundab	:	Recommended
Muslim	:	Believers in one God and the Prophet Mohamed (Sal). One who submits to the Will of God.
Muttaqin	:	Those who have Taqwa or fear of Allah.
Qiblah	:	Kiblah, The direction (toward the Kabah in Makkah) all Muslims must face when performing prayer from any given point on earth.

Quran	:	The final book or revelation from Allah to mankind, revealed to the Prophet Mohamed (Sal) over a span of 23 years.
Ral	:	Razhiallahu anhu (male) Razhiallahu anha (female) May Allah pleased with him or her.
Ramadan	:	Ninth month of the Islamic Calendar during which Muslims fast dawn to dusk.
Rasul Allah	:	Messenger of Allah-Prophet Mohamed (Sal).
Sabr	:	Observing patience.
Sadiq	:	The truthful.
Sahaba	:	Companions of the Prophet Mohamed (Sal) during his life.
Sal	:	Abbreviated words of honour and salutations attachedto the name of the Holy Prophet Mohamed (Sal). Meaning: May Allah send blessings and salutations on him.
Shariah	:	A path. It is used to mean Islam's legal system that Muslims abide by.
Shura	:	Consultation process of decision-making.
Sunnah	:	A tradition or practice. The body of traditions and practices of the Prophet (Sal); also includes his words, actions, or what has been approved by him.
Surah	:	A Chapter of the Quran.
Taqwa	:	Piety—fear of Consciousness of Allah.
Tawhid/Tauheed	:	The belief in the uniqueness of Allah.
Ummah	:	Refers to the community of believers worldwide, irrespective of colour, race, language, nationality or boundaries. The universal body of Muslims as a single community.
Wahy	:	Revelation from Allah.
Wajib	:	Obligatory

Yaqin : Conviction in Allah's signs.

Zakah : Poor due. The amount, at least 2.5 percent payable annually by a Muslim on his net savings as a part of his religious obligation, mainly for the benefit of the poor and the needy.

Zulm : Tyranny. A comprehensive term used to refer to all forms of inequity, injustice exploitation, oppression, and wrongdoing, whereby a person either deprives others of their rights or does not fulfil his obligations toward them.

Bibliography

Abdul Hakim, Khalifa (1987), The Prophet and His Message, Institute of Islamic Culture, Pakistan.

Ahmad, Fazl (1983), Omar The Second Caliph of Islam, Taj Company, Delhi.

Ahmed, H. Sheriff (1984), The Ideal Leadership : Bilal Muslim Mission, Kenya, pp. 9-11.

Al-Buraey, Muhammad (1985), Management and Administration in Islam, By Kegan Paul Interntional Ltd., UK, p. 348.

Altalib, Hisham (1993), Training guide for Islamic Workers, 3rd ed., The International Institute of Islamic Thought, USA.

Andrae, T., (1936), Mohammed : The Man and his Faith, George Allen and Unwin Ltd.

Ansari, M.A., (1986), Need for Nurturant Task Leaders in India; Some Empirical Evidence, *Journal of Management and Labour Studies*, 11, 26-36.

Argyle, M., G. Gardner and F. Cioffi (1958), Supervisory Methods Related to Productivity, Absenteeism and Labour Turnover, *Human Relations*, 11: 289-304.

Ayman, R. and M.M. Chemers (1983), Relationship of Supervisory Behaviour Ratings to work Group Effectiveness and Subordinate Satisfaction among Iranian Managers, *Journal of Applied Psychology*, 68: 338-41.

Azam, M.A., (1979), Leadership : Islamic Foundation, Bangladesh, Dacca, pp. 2-5.

Azzam, A.R., (1979), Life of Prophet Mohammed, The Islamic Foundation, Leicester.

Bangash, Zafar (2000), The Concept of Leader and Leadership in Islam : The Institute of Contemporary Islamic thought, London.

Barnlund, D.C. (1962), Consistency of Emergent Leadership in Groups with Changing Tasks and Members, *Speech Monographs*, 29: 45-52.

Bass, B.M. (1960), Leadership Psychology and Organisational Behaviour, New York, Harper.

Bass, B.M. (1985), Leadership and Performance Beyond Expectations. New York: Free Press.

Bass, B.M. and P.C. Burger (1979), Assessment of Managers: An International Comparison, New York: Free Press.

Bass, B.M., D.A. Waldman, B.J. Avolio and M. Bebb (1987), Transformational Leadership and the Falling Dominoes Effect, *Group and Organization Studies*, 12: 73- 87.

Beekun, Rafik and Jamal Badawi (1999), Leadership Process in Islam, Islamic Training Foundation, USA.

Beekun, Rafik and Jamal Badawi (1999), Leadership : An Islamic Perspective, Amana Publications, Maryland, USA.

Bennis, W.G., (1976), The Unconscious Conspiracy : Why Leaders Can't Lead, New York: AMACOM.

Bennis, W.G. and B. Nanus (1985), Leaders: the Strategies for Taking Charge, New York: Harper and Row.

Beri, J.C. (1976), Mechanisation, Employment Pattern and Productivity, *Indian Journal of Industrial Relations*, 11: 42 and 44.

Bond, M.H. and K.K. Hwang (1986), The Social Psychology of Chinese People, pp. 213-66, Hong Kong: Oxford University Press.

Bryman, A. (1986), Leadership and Organizations, London: Routeledge & Kegan Paul.

Bryman, A., M. Bresnen, J. Ford, A. Beardsworth and T. Keil (1987), Leader Orientation and Organizational Transience: An Investigation Using Fiedler's LPC Scale, *Journal of Occupational Psychology*, 60: 13-20.

Burns, J.M. (1978), Leadership, New York: Harper & Row.

Carlyle, T. (1907), Heroes and Hero Worship, Boston: Adams (first published 1841).

Chaudhari, *et al.* (1982), Patterns of Diversification in Larger Indian Enterprises, *Vikalpa*, 7: 23-39.

Cooper, R. (1966), Leader's Task Relevance and Subordinate Behaviour in Industrial Work Groups, *Human Relations*, 19: 57-84.

Dansereau, F.G., Graen and W. Haga (1975), A Vertical Dyad Linkage Approach to Leadership within Formal Organizations: A Longitudinal Investigation of the Role-making Process, *Organizational Behaviour and Human Performance*, 13: 46-78.

Davis, K., (1980), Human Behaviour at Work: Organizational Behaviour, Tata McGraw-Hill Publishing Co. Ltd., New Delhi.

Dholakia (1978), Relative Performance of Public and Private Manufacturing Enterprises in India. Total Factor Productivity Approach, *Economic and Political Weekly*, 13: M4-M11.

Dorwin Cartwright and Alvin Zender (1953), Group Dynamics, Research and Theory, New York: Harper & Row.

Dwivedi, R.S. (1979), Human Relations and Organisational Behaviour : A Global Perspective, Macmillan India Ltd, New Delhi, p. 372.

Dwivedi, R.S. (1982), Diagnosing and Managing Leadership Crisis among Indian Executives, *Lok Udyog*, November 1992, pp. 23-35.

Dwivedi, R.S. (1984), A Study of Some Behavioural Determinants of Organizational Performance in Public Enterprises, *Lok Udyog*, 18: 5-16.

Dwivedi, R.S. (2001), Human Relation and Organisational Behaviour—A Global Perspective: Macmillan India Ltd. p. 492.

Eldersveld, S.J., *et. al.*, (1961), Research in Political Behaviour, in S. Sidney Ulmer, ed., Introductory Reading in Political Behaviour, Chicago: Rand McNally & Co.

Etizioni, Amitai (1961), Complex Organizations. New York: Holt, Rinehart & Winston.

Farah, C.E., (1967), Islam: Beliefs of Observance, Barran's Educational Series, New York.

Farris, G.F. and D.A. Butterfield (1972), 'Control Theory in Brazilian Organization', *Administrative Science Quarterly*, 17: 574-85.

Fiedler, F. (1967), A Theory of Leadership Effectiveness, McGraw-Hill : New York.

Fleishmen, E.A. and J. Simmons (1970), Relationship Between Leadership Patterns and Effectiveness Ratings in Israeli Foreman, *Personal Psychology*, 23: 169-72.

Galton, F. (1870), Hereditary Genies, New York: Appleton.

Ganesh (1984), Performance of Management Education Institutions: An Indian Sampler, *International Studies of Management and Organisation*, 14: 197-217.

Gardner, H.W. and Gardner, M.J., (1981), Child and Development, Little Brown, Boston.

George O. Terry (1977), Principles of Management, Richard D. Irwin, Homewood, 1977.

Gibb, C.A., (1954), Leadership, in Gardner Lindzey, ed., *Handbook of Social Psychology*, Cambridge, Mass : Addition-Wesley.

Greertz, C. (1973), The Interpretation of Cultures, New York: Basic Books.

Habibullah, A.H.M. and J.B.P. Sinha (1980), Motivational Climate and Leadership Styles, *Vikalpa*, 5.

Haire, M., E.F. Ghiselli and L.W. Porter (1966), Managerial Thinking: An International Study, New York: Wiley.

Hangrove, E.C., (1966), Presidential Leadership Personality and Political Style : Collies Macmillan, London.

Hart, Michael (1979), The 100: Ranking of the Most Influential Persons in History, Golden Book Center, p. 33.

Heller, F.A. and B. Wilpert (1981), Competence and Power in Managerial Decision-making, Chichester: Willey.

Hemant Kumar Sabat (1998), New Era of Leadership, *Indian Management*, July, p. 81.

Heresy, P. and K.H. Blanchard (1982), Management of Organizational Behaviour; Utilizing Human Resources, Englewood Cliffs, NJ: Prentice-Hall.

Heresy, P. and Kenneth, H. Blanchard (1988), Management of Organizational Behaviour Utilizing Human Resources, Printice-Hall International, Inc., USA.

Hermasi, E., (1972), Leadership and National Development in North Africa, University of California Press, Berkley.

Hingar, Asha, (1984), Psychometric Verification of Leadership Styles, Indian Management, September, pp. 11-19.

Hofstede, G. (1980), Culture's Consequences: International Differences in Work-related Values. Beverly Hills, CA: Sage.

House, R.J. and T.R. Mitchell (1974), Path-Goal Theory of Leadership, *Journal of Contemporary Business*, 3: 81-97.

Husein Haykal (1993), The Life of Muhammed: English Translation by Ismail Raji al-faruqi, Kualalumpur.

Ibn, Khaldun (1967), The Muqaddimah : An Introduction to History, 3 Vols., 2nd edn, trans. by Franz Rosenthal, Bollingdon Foundation, New York.

IDE International Research Group (1981), Industrial Democracy in Europe, Oxford: Oxford University Press.

Izetbegovic, A.A., (1990), Islam Between East and West, 2nd edn. American Publications, Indianapolis.

Jabnoun, Naceur (2001), Islam and Management, International Islamic Publishing House, Riyadh, Saudi Arabia.

Ja'far Sheikh Idris (2002), Democracy *v.* Shura, YM Online Discussion Forum.

Jauharilal (1983), Leadership Styles and Decision-making: The Indian Context, *Indian Management*, Oct. 13-24.

Jawdal Sa'eed (1983), Work a Skill and a Will, Damascus, p. 29.

Khadra, Bashir (1990), The Prophetic-Caliphal Model of Leadership: An Empirical Study, Int. Studies of Management and Organisation, Vol. 20, No. 3, pp. 37-51, M.E. Sharp, Inc.

Kalim Siddiqui (1998), Political Dimensions of the Seerah : The Institute of Contemporary Islamic thought, London.

Kandhlawi, Muhammad Yusuf (1985), The Lives of the Sahabah (An English Translation of "*Hayatus Sahaba*" originally in Arabic, Idara Isha'at-e-Diniyat (P) Ltd., New Delhi, Vol. 2.

Katz, D. N. Maccoby, *et. al.* (1951), Productivity, Supervision and Morale Among Railroad Workers, Ann Arbor, Survey Research Centre, University of Michigan.

Katz, D. and R.L. Kahn (1953), Leadership Practices in Relation to Productivity and Morale in D. Cartwright and A. Zander (eds.) Group Dynamics, Peterson and Company.

Kegan, R. (1982), The Evolving Self: Problem and Process in Human Development, Cambridge, M.A: Harvard University Press.

Kegan, R. and Lahey, L.L. (1984), Adult Leadership and Adult Development : A Constructive View. in B. Kellerman (Ed).

Kenny, D.A. and S.J. Zacarro (1983), An Estimate of Variance Due to Traits in Leadership, *Journal of Applied Psychology*, 68 678-85.

Koontz, Harold, and O'Donnell, Cyril (1972), Principles of Management: An analysis of Managerial Functions, McGraw Hill Book Company Inc., Tokyo, 1972.

Kotter, J.P. (1982), The General Managers. New York: Free Press

Kuhnert, K.W and P. Levis (1987), Transactional and Transformational Leadership : A Constructive Developmental Analysis, *Academy of Management Review*, 12: 648-657.

Kuhnert, K. W. (1990), *Journal of Management*, Vol. 16, No. 3 pp. 599-600

Lakey, L., Souraine, E., Kegan, R. Goodman, R. and Flex, S. (1988), A guide to the subject object interview: Ibs Administration and Interpretaion, Cambridge, M.A: Harvard University, *Journal of Management*, Vol. 16 No. 3: 599-600.

Lall (1982), The Emergence of Third World Multinationals: Indian Joint Ventures Overseas, *World Development*, 10: 127-46

Lewin, K.R. Lippitt and R.K. White (1939), Patterns of Aggressive Behaviour in Experimentally Created Social Climates, *Journal of Social Psychology*, 10: 271-99.

Lewis, H., (1960), The Arabs in History, 2nd edn., Harper and Brothers, New York.

Liden, R.C. and G.B. Graen (1980), 'Generalizability of the Vertical Dyad Linkage Model of Leadership; *Academy of Management Journal*, 23: 451-65.

Likert, R. (1961), New Patterns of Management, New York: McGraw-Hill.

Linda, Smircich (1983), Concept of Organisational Analysis, *Administrative Science Quarterly*, Sept., p. 342.

Lord, R.G., C.L. de Vader and G.M. Alliger (1986), 'A Meta-Analysis of the Relation Between Personality Traits and

Leadership Perceptions: An application of Validity Generalization Procedures', *Journal of Applied Psychology*, 71: 402-10.

Maheshwari (1980), Decision Styles and Organisational Effectiveness, New Delhi: Vikas Publishing House.

Mahmoud Dhaouadi (1990), A Critical assessment of the Issues of Objectivity and Subjectivity in Contemporary Western Socio-Behavioural Thought and its Muslim Khaldunian Counterpart: *The American Journal of Islamic Social Sciences*, Vol. 7, No. 2, p. 201.

Malhotra, V. (1998), 'All Fired Up and Ready to lead', *The Economic Times*, 18 January, p. 13.

Mann, R.D. (1959), 'A Review of the Relationships Between Personality and Performance in Small Groups', *Psychological Bulletin*, 56: 241-70.

Mannheim, B.F., Y. Rim and G. Grinberg (1967), 'Instrumental Status of Supervisor as Related to Workers' Perceptions and Expectations', *Human Relations*, 20: 387-97.

Maudoodi, Sayyid, Abu A'la (1991), The Islamic Movement: Dynamics of Values, Power and Change, The Islamic Foundation, U.K.

Maudoodi, Sayyid Abul A'la (2000), Towards Understanding Islam, Markazi Maktaba Islami Publishers, New Delhi, p. 10.

Menon, S.K. (1975), Leadership and Effective Performance, Shri Ram Centre for Industrial Relations and Human Resources, New Delhi.

Meindl, J.R. and S.B. Ehrlich and J.M. Dukerich (1985), The Romance of Leadership, *Administrative Science Quarterly*, 30: 78-102.

Mintzberg, H. (1983), Power in and Around Organizations, Englewood Cliffs, NJ: Prentice-Hall.

Misumi, J. (1985), The Behavioural Science of Leadership (ed. M.F. Peterson), Ann Arbor, Michigan: University of Michigan Press.

Mohamed al-Asi (2000), The Prophet and Power: The Institute of Contemporary Islamic thought, London.

Mohamed al-Asi and Zafar Bangash (2000), The Seerah: A Power Perspective: The Institute of Contemporary Islamic Thought, London.

Morgan (1980), Paradigms, Metaphors and Puzzle Solving in Organizational Theory, *Administrative Science Quarterly*, 25: 605-22.

Moten, Rashid, A., (1989), Izlamization of Knowledge: Methodology of Research in Political Science, *The American Journal of Islamic Social Sciences*, Vol. 7, No. 2, 1990, pp. 162-64.

Muhammad Yusuf Islahi (2000), Etiquette of Life in Islam : Markazi Maktaba Islami Publishers, New Delhi, pp. 220, 323.

Muqim, Mohammad, (Editor) (1994), Research Methodology in Islamic Perspective, Institute of Objective Studies, New Delhi.

Murad, Khurram (1981), Islamic Movement in the West, Leicester, UK: The Islamic Foundation.

Musleh-uddin, M., (1999), Islam and its Political System, International Islamic Publishers, Delhi.

Multiyear and Vijaya Kumar (1985), Leadership Styles, Perceived Need Satisfaction and Subjective Job Characteristics Among Scientific Personnel, *Indian Journal of Industrial Relations*, 21: 173-97.

Parukh, S.K., (1995), The Leadership Conundrum, Indian Management, October, p. 39.

Patrick R. Penland (1974), Group Dynamics and Individual Development, New York: Dekker.

Peter B. Smith and Mark F. Peterson (1988), Leadership, Organizations and Culture, SAGE Publications, London.

Peterson, M.F., H. Maiya and C. Herreid (1987), 'Field Application of Japanese PM Leadership Theory in Two US Service Organisations', Unpublished manuscript, College of Business, Texas Tech. University, Lubbock TX.

Peterson, M.F., P.B. Smith and M.H. Tayeb (1987), 'Development and use of English Language Versions of Japanese PM Leadership Measures in Electronic Plants', Proceedings of the Annual Meeting of the Southern Management, Association, New Orleans, November 1987.

Quradawi, Y.A., (1960), The Lawful and Prohibited in Islam, Hindustan Publication.

Qutb, Muhammad (1982), Islam the Misunderstood Religion, Markazi Maktaba Islami, Delhi.

Reddin, W.J., (1967), The 3-D Management Style Theory, *Training and Development Journal*, April.

Rensis Likert (1961), New Patterns of Management, McGraw-Hill : New York.

Robert, R. Blake and Jane S. Mouton (1964), The Managerial Grid, Houston, Tex : Gulf Publishing Company.

Riaz Khan, M. (2002), Shura and Islamic Vision of Democracy, Message International.

Ritz, G. (1984), Sociological Theory, New York: Alfred Knopf, pp. 121-57.

Robbins, S.P., (1979), Organizational Behaviour: Concepts and Controversies, Englewood Cliffs, New Jersey, Prentice-Hall, Inc., p. 240.

Robert, R. Blake *et al.* (1964), 'Breakthrough in Organizational Development', *Harvard Business Review*, November-December, p-136.

Robert Tannanbaum and Warren H. Schmidt (1973), 'How to Choose a Leadership Pattern', *Harvard Business Review*, May-June.

Sadek Jawad Sulaiman (1999), The Shura Principle in Islam., Al-Hawar Center, Inc.

Sadler, P.J. (1970), 'Leadership Style, Confidence in Management and job satisfaction', *Journal of Applied Behavioural Science*, 6: 3-20.

Safi, Louay (1995), Leadership and Subordination : An Islamic Perspective, *The American Journal of Islamic Social Sciences*, Volume 12.

Schriescheim, C.A., Tolliver, J.M., and Behling, O.C. (1978), Leadership Theory : Some Implications for Managers, MSU Topics, (26).

Schumacher, E.F. (1978), A Guide for the Perplexed, Harper Colphon Books, New York.

Sinamovic, Ermin (2002), Democracy and the Majority Principle in Islamic Legal Political Thought, The Message International, Jamaica, April/May.

Singh, R. (1983), Leadership Style and Reward Allocation: Does Least Preferred Coworkers Scale Measure Task and Relation Orientation?, *Organizational Behaviour and Human Performance*, 32: 178-97.

Singh, J.P., (1990), Managerial Culture and Work-related Values in India, *Organizational Studies*, pp. 75-101.

Singh, P. and G.S. Das (1977), Managerial Style of Indian Managers: A Profile, *ASCI Journal of Management*, September, pp. 1-11.

Singh and Bhandarkar (1990), Corporate Success and Transformational Leadership, New Delhi: Wiley Eastern Ltd.

Sinha, T.N. and J.B.P. Sinha (1977), Differential Profile of Three Types of Leaders, A.N.S. Institute of Social Studies (Monograph), Patna.

Sinha, J.B.P. (1981), The Nurturant Task Manager: A Model of the Effective Executive, Atlantic Highlands, NJ Humanities Press.

Sinha, J.B.P. (1984), A Model of Effective Leadership Styles in India, *International Studies of Management and Organisation*, 14: 86-98.

Smith, W.C., (1957), Islam in Modern History, The New American Library, New York.

Stogdill, R.M. (1948), Personal factor's Associated with Leadership, A survey of the Literature; *Journal of Psychology*, 25: 35-71.

Stogdill, R.M. and A.E. Coons (eds.) (1957), Leader Behaviour: Its Description and Measurement, Columbus, OH: Bureau of Business Research, Ohio State University.

Stogdill, R.M. (1974), Handbook of Leadership, New York: Free Press.

Sulaiman, S.J., (1999), The Shura Principle in Islam, Al-Hewar Center, Inc. USA.

Taha Jabir al Alwani (1993), Source Methodology in Islamic Jurisprudence, English Edn. By Yusuf Talal Delorenzo and Anas S. al Shaikh-Ali, International Institute of Islamic Thought, USA, pp. 12-13.

Tannenbaum (1961), Leadership and Organization, McGraw-Hill, New York.

Terman, L.M. (1904), A Preliminary Study of the Psychology and Pedagogy of Leadership, *Journal of Genetic Psychology*, 11: 413-51.

The Alim, Islamic Software, (1986) ISL Software Corporation, USA.

Uma, R.V. (2000), Leadership and Organisational Effectiveness: A Study based on Selected Organisations, University of Madras.

Valdas Anelauskar (1999), Discovering America as it is : Clarity Press, Atlanta, USA, pp. 61-66.

Vroom, V.H. and A.G. Jago (1978), On the Validity of the Vroom-Yetton Model, *Journal of Applied Psychology*, 63: 151-62.

Watt, M.W., (1972), Muhammed : Prophet and Statesman, Oxford University Press, London.

Weber, M., (1947), The Theory of Economic and Social Organisation, New York: Free Press.

Weber, M., (1949), The Methodology of Social Sciences, Chicago: Free Press.

Whyte, W.F. and L.K. Williams (1963), Supervisory Leadership: An International Comparison, unpublished paper cited in A.S. Tannenbaum, *Organizational Psychology*, pp. 280-334.

Yahya, Abu Zakariya (1987) Riyadh-us-saleheen, (Arabic-English), Kitab Bhavan New Delhi.

Yukl, G.A. (1981), Leadership in Organizations, Englewood Cliffs, NJ: Prentice-Hall.

Yukl, G. and D. Van Fleet (1982), Cross-situational, Multi-method Research on Military Leader Effectiveness, Organisational Behaviour and Human Performance, 30: 87-108.

Zakariah, Muhammed (1979), The Teachings of Islam, Idara Isha'at-e-Diniyat (P) Ltd., New Delhi.

Index